Parties

Parties

a guide to successful party giving

Edited by Maggie Black

WARD LOCK LIMITED · LONDON

First published in Holland
© Meijer Pers N.V. Amsterdam
ISBN 0 7063 1084 5
First English edition published in Great Britain 1973
by Ward Lock Limited, 116 Baker Street,
London, W1M 2BB

Translated by Antonia Speller

Recipes created by Wina Born, Lily van Pareren and
Hugh Jans
Photographs by Ed Suister
Illustrations by Hugh Jans

Text filmset in 9 on 11 pt Univers

Printed and bound in Great Britain by
Cox & Wyman Ltd, London, Fakenham and Reading

There is hardly anything more personal than a party. We all arrange gatherings in our own special way — and that is how it should be. After all, parties provide an outlet for our own creativity, fantasy and joie de vivre.

This is why this book does not provide set rules and regulations, which would only hinder the preparation of your own celebration. What you will find are a number of tips which may spark off your own ideas, and a number of recipes which should encourage your curiosity.

There are tips for the universal celebrations, such as engagement and marriage, Christmas, and Easter, and also for the less usual parties: a festive barbecue, a gay picnic, a house-warming party, to mention only a few.

The same applies to the recipes. You will find here simple ones for the more popular celebrations, together with details you have probably never heard of before but which will be very worth while trying.

All this has one aim in mind: to help you to put your own signature on your party; to make it a celebration which will become your very own by giving it your personal touch in such a way that even months later your guests will retain happy memories.

We wish you great success.

contents

so you're going to give a party

Small and intimate parties, family parties, parties for friends and acquaintances, children's parties, a 'non-birthday' party, the 'surprise' party, an official party, gala parties — in our language just a few short words indicate such a multitude of different forms of the simple word 'party'.

Whether you decide to give a party to celebrate something specific, or for no reason than because you are in the mood for one, this by itself is a good enough reason to start your preparations, because they also are a part of the celebration. Whatever the party — to be successful it must be well prepared and well organized.

Only the so-called 'surprise' parties are exempt from this golden rule. At this kind of party, you as the chosen host or hostess are the more or less willing victim of a sudden invasion by your friends. You may even happen to be fast asleep; if so, you are rudely awakened. To avoid being a spoilsport — there really is no other way out — you may just ask for a short delay to make yourself ready, but after that you just let the 'surprise' party happen! Enjoy the unexpected occasion, even though you know that the clearing up afterwards will be a mighty task. It is better to put this out of your mind since the thought may be depressing.

As a good host or hostess, you should be able to cope with any situation like this. But if you would like the reputation of being a perfect hostess, then all your other parties must be planned ahead on paper. All good party-giving is mainly a question of organization and that is best done with pen and paper. So, to start with, buy a large pad and write down the reason for the party; birthday, engagement, marriage, success in an examination or whatever it may be. Then note down the type of party you want to give and which people you want to invite; plan the number of guests in accordance with the space available. Write down whether it is going to be a sit-down meal, a running buffet, a supper, extensive drinks, an evening party, an outdoor party or a pleasant lunch.

You can then decide what to offer your guests, depending on the type of party. Start jotting down dishes which may fit into the programme, and slowly but surely you will compose a menu for a dinner, an array for a cold buffet, an original luncheon or a series of exquisite tit-bits to go with drinks. You notice . . . you still need pen and paper.

One good piece of advice: give yourself plenty of time. It is important that you consider all possibilities. You must be sure, for example, that the people you invite are suited to one another, so that pleasant contacts are made.

For dinner, it is a convention to have an equal number of male and female guests; a well-mixed dinner party is usually a great success. Whatever the party, try not to have more than one woman 'spare'; a surplus of men is quite acceptable at any party where one does not formally sit around a table.

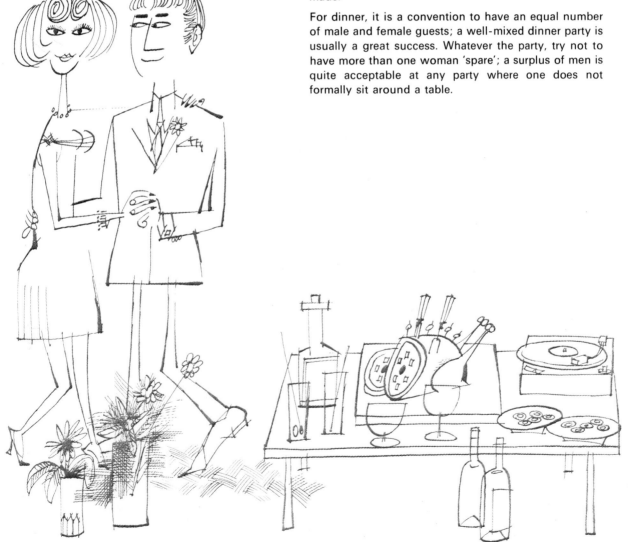

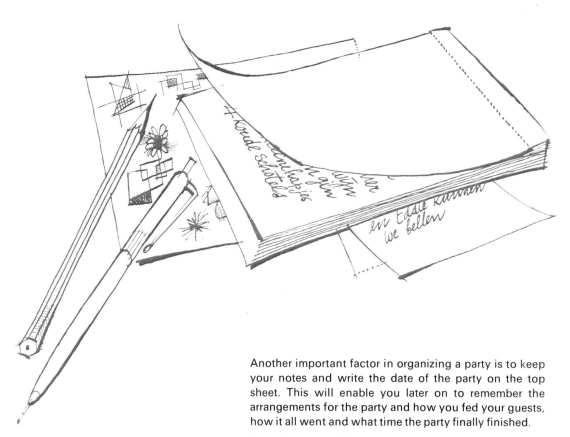

Another important factor in organizing a party is to keep your notes and write the date of the party on the top sheet. This will enable you later on to remember the arrangements for the party and how you fed your guests, how it all went and what time the party finally finished.

From this you will learn what to avoid in future, which dishes were a success and which combinations of people proved compatible.

You can invite people to a party in various ways. The most informal is an invitation by telephone, such as: 'We are going to give a party on such and such a day: can we count on your company?' — followed by some explanatory talk when you make it clear that it is not going to be at all formal: 'only some pleasant people we are getting together to have something to eat and drink'. If your girl friend touches on the subject of what to wear, your response should be: 'Oh just put on something easy, it really is not important.'

This, of course, lays down the rule for you as well, as a good hostess never outshines her guests; if in fact you mean to wear your latest and most expensive long creation, then it is a good idea to prepare your guests so that they have a chance to preen their most colourful feathers and the men do not appear in jeans or Wild-West sweaters.

If the party is to celebrate a birthday or any other special event, you must inform your guests. Some of them will know already and will want to bring you a suitable present. However, the people who can not possibly know, and who are not informed by you for reasons of false modesty, may feel a bit upset, and such a situation must be avoided by a good hostess.

For more official occasions, a written invitation is appropriate. If it is a silver wedding or similar celebration when just family and friends are being invited, the couple concerned usually write a personal invitation to attend the dinner, luncheon or whatever is organized. Only on a very official occasion is a printed invitation used.

Naturally, the invited guest should reply as soon as possible to let the hostess know whether or not he or she can accept the invitation.

The procedure for children's parties is usually a bit different. Then the mothers contact one another, either by telephone or in writing. Also, for these parties there are some other rules which should be observed. It must be made perfectly clear where the party is going to take place, whether one intends to take the children out and how the transport has been arranged (do not forget to ask whether there are any objections) and at what time the young guest can be collected. Also do remember to say whether or not the children will have a light meal, and reassure the parent that they will not be provided with masses of sticky sweets.

If you are giving the party for older children, they can send their own invitations, which they can either draw or decorate themselves. The children are then involved in the preparations and they usually love it. For a children's party, careful preparations are even more essential than for adults. After all, children must be entertained. Do not let them get out of hand, or play

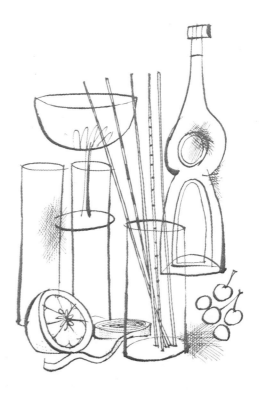

over-riotous games; the result can easily be either quarrelling or mischief.

After a really successful party, the children will return home enthusiastic and full of tales, but as a rule the parents of the young host or hostess are usually worn out and deserve a day of rest afterwards to recover.

This is why many parents nowadays decide to organize something out of doors: a visit to the zoo, the panto-mime, or to a special children's play are great favourites. If you decide on this escape route, plenty of adult assistance is essential, their numbers depending on the size of the party: two adults who have to look after twenty-five sturdy youngsters in a zoo are usually at the end of their tether after a quarter of an hour, not because the children are particularly naughty but because everything they see or experience fascinates them to such an extent that they completely forget their en-vironment. It would be a disaster if one of your small guests crawled underneath the fence because the lions were 'such sweet pussycats' and he does not realize that the cats might see in him a juicy tit-bit.

Whatever your party, take care that you yourself welcome your guests and introduce them to one another. This is a friendly gesture, and nobody nowadays has the perfect manservant or a parlourmaid to announce them even at formal parties. Follow the greeting with the introductions at once. If everybody already knows everybody else, there are no problems, but this is usually not the case. Introductions can sometimes be difficult because the names are drowned in the noise. This is why it is quite correct for a guest when talking afterwards to a person to whom he has been introduced, to ask him to repeat his name.

Naturally, you will provide every new arrival with food and drink, and it is your task as the hostess to see that the newcomer enters a pleasant circle. It is sometimes important for you to know not only the professions of your guests, but also their hobbies; in this way you can encourage pleasant small-talk. Between ourselves, a hostess should be compared with a centipede; she must have eyes and feelers everywhere to make sure that her guests are enjoying themselves.

If you suspect that one of your guests is a little shy, why not engage her as your special aid? It will make all the contacts easier and your own task a little lighter. However, as soon as you see that the shy person is absorbed in the festive atmosphere, disengage her from her tasks, with a kind word of thanks if it is suitable.

If you are giving the party in a flat or in a terrace or semi-detached house, be tactful and inform your neighbours beforehand. You cannot give a party without a noise, and if your neighbours know beforehand what is going on, they can take any necessary precautions either to go out or not to be disturbed by the performance. If they are your friends invite them too; that avoids any possible trouble and 'a good neighbour is always better than a remote friend.'

Obviously, guests have some obligations too. The golden rule applies to everyone; know your own alcoholic capacities and remain well within your limit. Remember, an important problem in our modern society is drink and driving. Also avoid eating too much, with all the nasty consequences. A guest who becomes sleepy and disinterested because he has over-enjoyed the goods of this earth, is in fact a bad guest.

A good hostess always provides an array of pleasant non-alcoholic drinks for drivers; the good guest often leaves his car at home so that he can enjoy the fare without remorse.

Again, it may happen that a person cannot have alcoholic drinks for health reasons. A good hostess provides fruit juice, or a non-alcoholic aspect is not emphasized. In this way troublesome interest from others is avoided: at a party, one's own and other people's health should not be a topic of conversation.

Never insist if a person does not want to eat or drink some particular thing, and do not consider him as a miracle if he has recently stopped smoking. It may be more difficult for him than you imagine, so do not add to his problem. If it does *not* cause him difficulties, the fuss is only a bore to him.

When you start organizing a party, divide your organization into three parts: the arrival of the guests and getting the party going; the part when you have to supervise the party's progress, and finally the last part when the guests prepare to leave.

A drawn-out party is often a failure; so it will be your task to determine the time of departure, and tactfully arrange it while everything is still fun. Your planned 'final piece' will depend of course on the type of party, but the actual departure of the guests must also have your full attention. Make sure you say goodbye to everybody personally, and if possible escort them to the front door (or, if you have a flat, to the lift door).

Try, too, to see that everybody has transport, and that any single woman is taken home. You may be able to arrange her transport by car with other guests; otherwise, order a taxi and accompany her to it. An extra courtesy is to enquire next day whether she arrived home safely. However independent a single woman is, such attention is always appreciated.

When the guests have departed, both host and hostess are likely to be tired out, but do try to start the cleaning up. Really it is the best thing to do; there is no greater nightmare than the party debris 'the morning after the night before'. Gather your flagging spirits in a last brave attempt; make a strong cup of coffee and commence battle. You will probably have to do this anyhow, (a) if the party has been rampant throughout the house, (b) because any borrowed items will have to be returned as soon as possible, both washed and packed. Many a nightly hour has been spent by party-givers in washing and cleaning up. However, when finally you crawl into bed, your conscience will be clear.

preparations for the party

So, here you are, sitting with a clean, empty pad, because you intend to give a party soon. It may be for some special occasion; on the other hand, there may be no reason at all.

First, in determining what type of party you wish to give, remember that the arrangement of your home plays an important part in it. Maybe your home has the dimensions of a palace and your dining-room is enormous. In this case, a dinner with several courses is possible. However, if you only occupy a small modern flat with a tiny kitchen, forget your formal dinner, and concentrate on light 'refreshments'. On the other hand, suppose you have an old-fashioned large kitchen or a modern kitchen–dining-room – these are ideal if you want to serve a cold buffet. Hide as many pots and pans as possible. The kitchen dresser, provided it is covered with a tablecloth, is admirably suited to display made-up dishes.

A very attractive decor can be arranged by placing the different platters at various heights. Use shoe-boxes or even piles of books and hide them with crêpe paper. Place some candles on the shelves and some flowers in jars, pots or vases. They can look very attractive.

If there is not enough room for plates and cutlery, put these on a separate small table. For the rest, clear as much as possible out of the kitchen, arrange a colourful decoration, provide flattering lighting and you will be amazed at the effect.

A kitchen party like this has the added advantage that any hot soup you intend to provide can be served straight from the cooker. If you serve a running buffet with it, remember that the portions must be small, so that they can be eaten 'in one go'. Do not impose on your guests beautifully decorated open sandwiches which entirely disintegrate because the slices of meat cannot be bitten through; and with any food which is served to be eaten on the lap, you must serve a complete set of cutlery, wrapped in a paper napkin. While soft ones are the most pleasant to use, the smaller, thinner ones can be folded elegantly in wine-glasses and placed in various strategic positions for the guests to help themselves. If a particular colour combination is carried throughout the decorations, the effect will be quite spectacular. Perhaps the flowers can tone in, and even some of the dishes you serve.

Most people nowadays do not have enough china for a really big party. Some firms hire out, at quite a reasonable price, tables, chairs, china, cutlery and even hall-stands, a bar and any enormous pans you may need, in addition to large platters, glasses, and wine coolers.

This is why it is so essential to determine at an early stage what kind of a party yours will be. Complete lists must be drawn up of any items you plan to hire; make one copy to be sent to the firm and one copy to keep yourself. Order everything for early delivery, because the unpacking and washing-up before use is quite time-absorbing. All the smaller articles will probably be in crates packed in straw and paper and immediately upon receipt you should inform the supplier of any errors and breakages as they can then still be put right. Enquire

about the regulations concerning breakage, so that you know precisely where you are. Also arrange when everything should be collected again.

Your floral decoration should also be worked out at an early stage and ordered accordingly. If you are good at arranging flowers yourself, you will probably make your own display but if not, there are many possibilities for decoration which do not require flowers. Crêpe paper is the medium 'par excellence' and craft shops stock numerous colours. Calculate beforehand approximately how much you will need. Most stationery shops also have an extensive range of menu cards, invitation cards and similar useful party aids.

the comfort of the guests

Physical comfort for your guests is essential for the right party atmosphere. Use your own bedroom for a ladies' cloakroom and arrange it as a room where they can retire for a while, if you give a large party. If you have a dressing-table, remove your personal toiletries and provide:

safety pins, hair clips and lacquer spray, a clean comb, a hand mirror, powder, two or three lipsticks, eyeshadow, cotton wool and tissues, aspirin and a water jug and glass.

Put an adequate supply of clean guest towels near the wash-basin in the bathroom. A very thoughtful hostess may even provide means to deal with unexpected menstrual accidents and one or two cheap toothbrushes. She will certainly remember ashtrays, matches and cigarettes. The bathroom must also be provided with a new tablet of soap. A sign on the door lets your guests know where they can retire to refresh themselves.

lists for suppliers

As soon as you have decided what food and drink and entertainment you will give your guests, draw up lists for the suppliers. This is to make sure that everything will arrive at your home in time.

Whatever kind of party you plan, choose dishes which are simple and the ingredients of which are readily available. Do not experiment with concoctions you have not tried out before or the outcome of which is unknown to you, unless you plan a general rehearsal beforehand. Avoid dishes which must be served at precisely the right moment, even if you determine the time at which certain events are to take place.

As for the drinks, it is not necessary to stock a great variety to meet all possible requests of your guests. If you are going to have a bar, a good solution is to hang up a list with all available drinks or combinations you intend to provide. Inform the person in charge of the bar of the number of drinks you have allowed for each guest as a rough guide. This is another reason why timing your programmes is important: you can discourage the downing of pre-dinner drinks when the meal and wine are about to be served.

a party with a game

If you organize a party which does not consist only of 'eats', drinks and talk (such as a bridge-drive, a dance or a car rally) you must think of the necessary requirements and arrange the details beforehand.

A 'treasurehunt' by car with various tasks to be completed is one kind of party which is usually a great success. The trail usually ends at the hostess's home, and the prize-giving is followed by drinks and something to eat to round off the event. Usually the hostess herself does not participate in the 'hunt'. She welcomes the arrivals and takes care that the final celebration runs smoothly.

A bridge-drive must also be well prepared. Space tables well apart and have plenty of new cards, and scoring pads. 'Eats' should be easy to eat, and not sticky. As for prizes for the winning team, do not make them too expensive. Originality is appreciated much more.

Have you ever thought of giving a large party in period costume? It is usually easily arranged, and you can 'tip off' your guests as to where they can borrow or hire costumes. A great variety of period dresses can be hired from stage costumiers and repertory theatres as well as the necessary wigs to complete the outfits. Modern people escape only too willingly from their own time for a brief encounter with the past. Remember though to adjust the food to the period you wish to bring alive again. For example, if your party concentrates on the 17th century, then you should provide large pies and beer in mugs. Of course, such a party is usually given only once in a lifetime; this is all the more reason to make it an outstanding success, and long remembered by your fortunate guests.

music is important

To make a party a success, keep any music as varied as possible. The most practical solution is often to have good dance music on tape. Vary the dance music with chansons and songs; in other words, choose music in tune with the party.

Don't let the music be so loud that it drowns all conversation.

If you use your own records on your record player, do arrange for someone who is careful to be in charge. Put any very precious L.P.s away for the night; this will avoid heart-ache afterwards. Never make the error of announcing in the middle of the festivities that the very latest classical record is about to be played, however much you and possibly one or two of your guests adore it. Music is decisive in determining the atmosphere of a party; it can make it or break it, and you will hush the gaiety. For a big party, sound-amplifying installations as well as tapes can be hired, but it is quite an expensive business.

party furniture

Again for a large party, very large damask tablecloths and serviettes can be hired, and for garden parties one can usually hire from a large-scale caterer elegant French garden furniture and 'romantic' lighting equipment.

help can be a boon

If it is necessary, say for a large official party, one can hire assistance. However, in most cases one can call in the help of a young girl friend for the occasion. Make the arrangement in good time and don't keep your voluntary help at work for the entire evening.

Do most of the preparations well in advance to make sure that the service will be easy and smooth. For example, if you are going to celebrate a birthday and have invited some friends for 'a drink with some food', forget about a conventional first course and replace it with a really good choice of tit-bits and colourful, made-up cold finger-food which can be prepared beforehand. Gradually, during the party, you can produce new full platters when you remove the empties to the kitchen.

Then, last, as a pièce de resistance, produce an imaginative hot casserole and oven-baked dessert.

The plates, cutlery rolled in the serviettes, the glasses and whatever else is required for these hot dishes are put aside in another room. Take care to have pleasant lighting, so that this room also forms a part of the celebrations.

Every guest helps himself to a plate and a set of cutlery and is either served by the hostess or serves himself. The host will be in charge of a suitable wine or will serve beer. The helpers have then a little time to collect, at great speed, all dirty glasses, plates, and to empty ashtrays, so that the first room is ready for use again when the time for the coffee has arrived. While everyone is occupied with their dessert, the coffee can be made. In this manner you will go through your set programme with an effortless grace, without any harassing rushing and running about.

It is very important that the guests receive the impression that everything takes place without any trouble. Any considerate guest will, of course, realize that gnomes no longer exist, and the result is often that, at the end of the party, there are helping hands to do the washing-up and clearing away.

If you have neither voluntary nor paid helpers, then you, and perhaps your husband and children, will have to clear up the mess. There are, of course, the 'advanced thinkers' who use disposable plates, dishes and bowls for reasons of simplicity. But this is only of limited help as all the glasses, the cutlery, ashtrays, etc. still have to be washed; moreover, this disposable 'china' is quite expensive if you entertain often.

the unexpected
party

To organize parties is a pleasant pastime. Yet to improvise parties can be even greater fun, as long as we enjoy the unexpected, a surprise, a pleasant event without any necessarily logical reason, just because the sun is shining, or perhaps is not shining, because you are young, or your birthday cake is graced with more than seventy candles. . . .

It may appear to be a contradiction, but even an unprepared party needs *some* prior preparation; even if it is only long-term preparation, which you can quietly forget until the time comes when something must be done at once. To be more precise: if you wish to be prepared, you must carry a stock of all kinds of items which are essential for a festive meal.

There may be some fortunate people whose freezer is graced with whole salmon or venison. Their problems are light — but such people are rare. Most of us have to manage with the ordinary household refrigerator and a very modest larder in which we can store, at most, some tins and packets. It then becomes true art to use our limited space to the best advantage, and so provide for all possibilities.

An 'eventuality' stock which might provide festive inspiration could include the following:

packets of quick-cooking rice and macaroni;
packets of powdered, concentrated soups, such as tomato (red), mushroom (white) and consommé (for aspics);
cans of fish, such as sardines, tuna and (if you feel extravagant) crab, lobster or oysters;
canned meats, such as ham, corned beef and cocktail frankfurters.

If you use cans of vegetables, keep garden peas and asparagus tips, and also cans of fruit (especially pineapple and pear). Keep also some bars of chocolate; then you can face any party hazard.

See, of course, that you also have eggs, cheese, double cream and tomato purée always available, and that for cases of emergency you have some cream crackers or other dry biscuits handy.

Naturally this list is incomplete and can be varied, as long as you see that the stock includes something in each group.

Here then are possibilities for an impromptu festive meal:

first courses

1   *Open sandwiches*; inspired by the Danish smörrebrød: for instance, smoked salmon with asparagus; hard-boiled eggs with sardines; slices of sausage with potato salad; ham, bacon or sausage with strips of green pepper; hard-boiled egg with slices of tomato.

2   *Italian antipasto*; place on a large platter a colourful combination of fish (sardines, tuna, shrimps) meat products (sausages, raw ham, salami), vegetables (salad, tomatoes, asparagus, or vegetable leftovers from a previous day marinated in oil and lemon juice); add hard-boiled egg, strips of cheese, or olives. Serve with rye bread or crisp toast for a change.

3   *Salads*; leftovers of boiled potato salad; salmon, garden peas or asparagus; mayonnaise, garnished with egg and tomato; tuna salad; green bell pepper; possibly a few finely sliced olives, mayonnaise or salad dressing; hard-boiled egg and tomato; Italian salad with potato, ham or sausage and various kinds of vegetables such as garden peas, carrots, asparagus, cauliflower and runner beans.

soup

4   *Soup*; tins of soup can simply be thinned and heated and decorated with, for instance, cream, crumbled hard-boiled egg (tomato soup), Madeira or sherry (oxtail soup); one can also combine, for instance, tomato soup and oxtail, or mushroom and tomato. Tomato soup can be made more luxurious by adding shrimps or finely cut crab and a little sherry.

main course

The simplest basis is rice or macaroni, with a thick and tasty sauce. Below we suggest some possibilities:

a undiluted tomato soup, garnished with some crab, shrimps, tuna or crayfish and a little cream;

b undiluted mushroom soup garnished with crab or shrimps and coloured with tomato purée;

c undiluted oxtail soup with ham or corned beef, flavoured with tomato purée or sherry;

d undiluted mushroom soup, well flavoured with curry, garnished with quickly fried onion and pieces of apple, ham (or crab) and topped with cream;

e undiluted tomato soup with plenty of quickly fried onion, fried bacon cubes, ham or corned beef.

The rice can be colourfully decorated by folding garden peas into it. If you have enough tomatoes, a tomato salad is always a favourite, but do not serve it with a sauce based on tomato soup. Mixed pickles can also be served with any spicy sauces.

If you do not like rice or macaroni make instead an instant potato purée, which can also be made more interesting with a savoury sauce. Also boiled potatoes in pots or tins are also ideal for serving in a tasty sauce as a kind of ragoût.

sweet course

Try one of these:

a tinned pears with hot chocolate sauce, made with chocolate bars with some strong black coffee and cream, melted over hot water;

b pineapple, flavoured with some port or Madeira;

c pineapple topped with grated chocolate, sprinkled with Madeira or rum, and wrapped in foil and placed for ten minutes in a hot oven.

a coffee or tea interlude

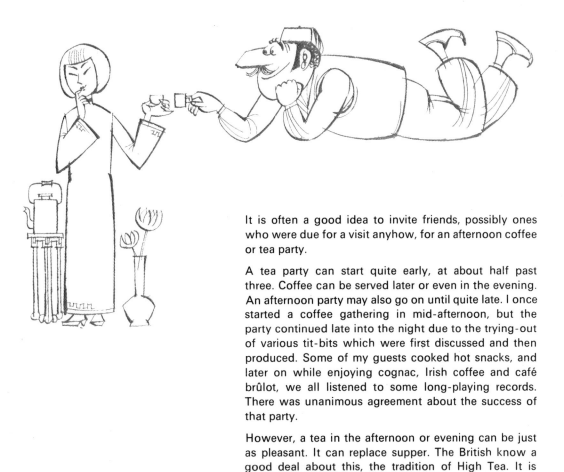

It is often a good idea to invite friends, possibly ones who were due for a visit anyhow, for an afternoon coffee or tea party.

A tea party can start quite early, at about half past three. Coffee can be served later or even in the evening. An afternoon party may also go on until quite late. I once started a coffee gathering in mid-afternoon, but the party continued late into the night due to the trying-out of various tit-bits which were first discussed and then produced. Some of my guests cooked hot snacks, and later on while enjoying cognac, Irish coffee and café brûlot, we all listened to some long-playing records. There was unanimous agreement about the success of that party.

However, a tea in the afternoon or evening can be just as pleasant. It can replace supper. The British know a good deal about this, the tradition of High Tea. It is really more like supper with one or more savoury dishes, as well as sandwiches, sweet biscuits, and cakes.

The tea drunk in Europe comes mainly from China, India, Ceylon and Indonesia, but Russia, Japan and parts of Africa and the United States also grow tea.

The manner of mixing teas, making and pouring it, fills a book in itself. I think it a good idea to have various types of tea in the house if you can; for example, have a good ordinary 'Indian' mixture, but also some 'Earl Grey' or 'Lapsang Souchong': alternatively, keep for luxury Jasmin tea from Hongkong or Young Chunmee green tea from the Chinese Republic.

For making any tea, use an ample teapot made of china or earthenware (it should hold approximately 3 pints) and rinse it with some freshly boiled water, in order to warm the pot. Throw this water away. Place spoonfuls of tea in the pot, and pour freshly boiled water on top. First pour only a little water in, and loosen, by rotating the pot, the first darkest essences of the tea leaves, then pour on the remaining boiling water. Put the lid on the pot and leave it to 'brew' for a few minutes. Then stir the tea with a spoon, and serve it.

Always use ample tea if it is 'Indian'; weak tea seldom refreshes or pleases. Do not think that by brewing it longer, you can use less tea. Long stewing only releases the tannic acid which gives the tea a bitter, acid flavour. Don't think either that a half-empty teapot only has to be refilled with boiling water in order to provide more tea. Make a new pot, or you will have a watery, weak product. Never rinse a teapot with soapy water. Rinse it with clear hot water.

On a long hot summer day, iced tea is refreshing. Serve it in a big jug with tinkling ice cubes and thin slices of lemon.

Now let us start our tea party with some recipes for different styles of tea and with some recipes of tit-bits to go with them.

TEA WITH RUM

freshly made tea for 8
people
sugar to taste
1 liqueur glass rum
1 slice of lemon for each glass

Fill the glass with tea in the usual way: add the sugar and pour the rum into the glasses. Place a thin slice of lemon on top of each drink and serve. You can serve it cold, but if you do, add a little more sugar. On really hot days, an ice cube in the tea will be appreciated.

RUSSIAN TEA

3½ teaspoons honey
1 piece of whole
   cinnamon
4 cloves
1 cup of water
2¾ pints water
10–12 teaspoons of tea
1 lemon
2 oranges

A glowing drink for ten cold Russians! Leave the honey, cinnamon and cloves to simmer in 1 cupful of water in a small saucepan for 10 minutes. Strain. Peel the thin yellow zest from one orange, and reserve it. Make the tea in the usual manner; add the strained spiced syrup together with the strained juice of the lemon and the oranges. Leave to simmer for 6 minutes. Serve the tea in glasses decorated with a piece of the orange peel zest.

PANDORA TEA

2¾ pints freshly made tea
   sugar to taste
1 tablespoon double cream
   per person
5 drops crème de menthe
   per person

Put into each glass 1 tablespoon whipped cream to which 5 drops of crème de menthe have been added. Pour the tea into the glasses, add the sugar and stir.

HOT TEA PUNCH

nearly 1½ pints freshly
   made tea
3 oranges
5¼ oz sugar
6 cups water
   mint leaves

Mix the freshly made tea with the juice of 3 oranges, the sugar and the water. Bring to boil and serve in punch glasses with 1 teaspoon finely chopped mint leaves for each glass.

AMERICAN ICED TEA

1¾ pints freshly made tea
1 lemon
   nearly ½ pint pineapple
   juice
1¾ oz sugar
   nearly ½ pint cold water
   ice cubes

Peel the lemon and reserve the peel. Mix the freshly made tea with the juice of the lemon, the pineapple juice and the sugar. Strain the liquid and leave to cool. Add the cold water and stir well. Serve in glasses with a cube of ice and piece of lemon peel on the edge of the glass.

A variety of festive food is described in the 'Concorde Recipe Book' about party dishes for tea party occasions. Below we describe a few more, which may come in useful.

SANDWICHES

On thin slices of white bread, serve one or more of the following:

EGG AND PORK

Crumble the yolks of hard-boiled eggs with a fork and mix in an equal weight of softened butter. Stir in some ½-inch cubes of pork or luncheon meat from a tin, and season the mixture with onion salt, pepper and a little nutmeg. Spread thin slices of a square tin loaf, which have been cut in half, with this tasty savoury.

CORNED BEEF WITH RÉMOULADE SAUCE

Cut thin slices of a square tin loaf diagonally across, cover with slices of meat and decorate with Rémoulade sauce, sprinkle with a little grated horseradish and finely chopped parsley.

On thin slices of wholemeal bread:

SALAMI AND OLIVES

Cover slices of wholemeal bread with thinly sliced, skinned salami and then some very thinly cut slices of raw onion. Decorate with halved and stoned olives and thin strips of greenbell pepper.

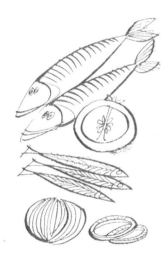

ONION AND OLIVES

Cover lightly toasted slices of brown bread with paper-thin rings of raw onion. Decorate with halved and stoned olives and thin strips of greenbell pepper.

ONION AND ANCHOVY

Cover lightly toasted slices of brown bread with paper-thin rings of raw onion. Place crosswise 2 strips of anchovy on top and garnish with 2 capers. Sprinkle the sandwich with a little freshly ground black pepper.

On thin slices of round rye bread:

SMOKED HERRING WITH TOMATO MAYONNAISE

Cover the rye bread with fillets of herring. Top it with thin slices of cucumber, and decorate with tomato mayonnaise made with a good-quality mayonnaise mixed with tomato ketchup, a little dry white wine and a few grains of paprika.

SAVOURY BLUE CHEESE SPREAD

Cover the rye bread with a paste made of blue cheese (Roquefort, Gorgonzola or Bresse Bleu) mixed with butter, milk, sherry, paprika and cayenne pepper to suit your taste.

Let us leave sandwiches at this point and focus instead on some hot snacks.

FRIED PRAWNS WITH MUSTARD MAYONNAISE FOR A CROWD

1 lb deep-frozen shelled
   prawns
1 mug of beer
   flour
   pepper
   salt
   garlic powder

for the sauce
$\frac{7}{8}$ pint mayonnaise
1 teaspoon mustard
1 teaspoon capers
$\frac{1}{2}$ tablespoon chopped
   gherkin
1 tablespoon chopped
   parsley

Thaw the prawns at room temperature, and marinate in a bowl filled with light beer. Drain. Toss them in the flour which has been seasoned with the pepper, salt and garlic powder. Deep-fry in hot olive oil. Place on soft paper so that the surplus oil can be absorbed. Mix the ingredients for the mustard mayonnaise and serve the cold sauce with the hot fried prawns.

MUSHROOMS ON TOAST

8 oz mushrooms
   olive oil
   pepper and salt
2 cloves of garlic, pounded
   to a paste
   paprika
1 glass dry white wine
2 bunches cleaned parsley
   oil for frying

De-stalk the mushrooms. Cut the large ones in halves and leave the small ones as they are. Cover the bottom of a large heavy frying pan with a thin layer of oil and heat slowly. The oil must be hot but no blue haze should appear. Place the mushrooms in the pan and fry them quickly until golden-brown, turning them over occasionally. When the mushrooms are half done, add the garlic and turn the mushrooms over again with a spatula. Sprinkle some paprika powder on top. Add the glass of white wine when the mushrooms are cooked and turn over once more. Serve with crisply fried sprays of parsley and freshly toasted bread.

Now let us pass on to two sweet recipes for a tea party.

MADEIRA CAKE

butter for greasing tin
flour for preparing tin
5¼ oz butter
5 oz granulated sugar
grated peel of ½ lemon
2 unbeaten eggs
5¼ oz flour
2 teaspoons baking powder
salt

Butter the inside of an oblong cake tin, about 10½ inches × 3 inches bottom and 2¾ inches high. Dust the inside of the tin with flour and shake out the surplus.

Mix the 5¼ oz butter and the sugar, the grated lemon peel and the salt to a smooth paste. Beat with an electric or rotary beater till the mixture is fluffy; add one egg at a time and continue beating until the mixture is well blended. The eggs should be at room temperature. Should the mixture separate, warm the outside of the bowl, add one tablespoon of the flour and mix until smooth.

Sift the flour and baking powder, and add gradually to the contents of the bowl. Beat in thoroughly, to blend. Heat the oven to 350° F, 180° C, gas 4. Fill the baking tin. Smooth the surface of the cake mixture, make a shallow channel lengthwise in the centre of the surface and push the sides a little upwards: this will result in a smooth and even surface on the cake. Place the cake in the centre of the oven and do not open the oven door for approximately 70 minutes. At the end of the baking time, test the cake with a hot metal skewer or a knitting needle; insert in the centre of the cake; if the needle is clean when it is drawn out, the cake is done. Remove the tin from the oven and leave to cool for a short time before removing the cake from the tin. Turn the cake out on to a rack so that it can cool on all sides.

It is a simple matter to introduce some variation into this basic recipe: The lemon peel can be replaced by orange or tangerine peel, or by grated crystallized ginger, raisins, or candied peel.

If you wish, sprinkle the cake with granulated sugar 5 minutes before the end of the baking time; or ice it with thin glacé icing when cold.

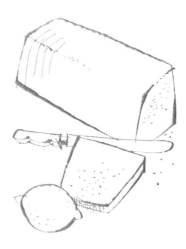

SHORTCRUST TART WITH APRICOT FILLING

8¾ oz flour with 2
 teaspoons baking
 powder or 8¾ oz
 self-raising flour
3½ oz butter
2½ oz soft brown sugar
1 egg
 salt
1 to 2 tablespoons water
 vanilla-flavoured sugar

Pre-heat the oven to 180° C, 350° F, gas 4. Place the dry ingredients in a bowl and mix carefully. Cut in the cold butter with two knives. Knead to form a ball. Do not over-knead; work the mixture just enough to shape the ball. During the kneading, add the egg and the water gradually. Leave the dough to firm up in a cool place. Roll the dough out on a lightly floured board to fit a cake tin about 8 inches in diameter and 2½ inches high. Place in the centre of the oven and bake for 20 to 25 minutes. Leave the tart to cool. Fill with apricot jam to which you have added a few halves of canned apricots and a small glass of crème de noyau or rum.

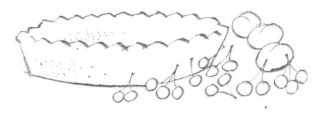

For a coffee party, I would like to give you some coffee drinks and then the recipe of a savoury dish which is certain to be a success. It will be an interesting novelty to add to the sweet snacks which you can buy, such as brioches, scones, rolls, and small cakes. This festive hot dish, made by yourself, will be your crowning glory. If you wish to serve cheeses, let them follow the hot dish.

First here are the drinks recipes:

CAFÉ BRÛLOT

1½ teaspoons ground allspice
1¼ pints freshly made coffee
⅓ cup castor sugar
 about ⅓ pint cognac
 peel of one orange cut
 into strips
 peel of one lemon cut into
 strips

Add the allspice to the coffee and leave covered for about a quarter of an hour. Strain the coffee and heat it again. In the meantime place the sugar, cognac, and the strips of peel in a small metal pan. Warm the pan and ignite the cognac. Slowly, pour it on the hot coffee. When the flames have subsided, pour the coffee into small cups.

PLANTER'S ICED COFFEE

1¼ pints freshly made coffee
6 oz sugar
5 liqueur glasses rum
juice of 1 lemon
crushed ice

Stir the sugar into the hot coffee until dissolved and leave it to cool. Add the rum and the lemon juice and pour into glasses with a tablespoon of crushed ice in the bottom of each. Serve ice cold.

Now here is that savoury pièce de resistance for your coffee party:

PRAWNS TEMPURA WITH SOUR-SWEET COFFEE SAUCE

¾ lb deep-frozen shelled prawns
6 oz sifted flour
1 teaspoon baking powder
½ teaspoon salt
1 egg
sour-sweet coffee sauce (see below)

Thaw the deep-frozen prawns at room temperature. Dry them well. Put flour, baking powder and salt through a sieve. Beat the eggs lightly, add the flour mixture and mix everything well. Add the water a spoonful at a time, and stir until the mixture is smooth and has the consistency of a paste.

Dip the prawns separately in the batter and deep-fry them in oil heated to 350–360° F until golden brown. Do not fry too many prawns at once. Place the prawns on soft paper so that the surplus oil is absorbed. Serve with the sour-sweet sauce below.

SOUR-SWEET SAUCE

½ teacup firmly packed brown sugar
1 tablespoon cornflour
¼ pint freshly made coffee
½ teacup vinegar
¼ teaspoon salt
2 tablespoons tomato ketchup
pepper
1 8-oz tin pineapple chunks
1 tomato cut in wedges
1 greenbell pepper, diced
1 tablespoon cooking oil

Mix the sugar and the cornflour. Stir in the coffee, then add the vinegar, salt, ketchup, pepper and pineapple. Stir on a moderate heat until the sauce thickens. Remove from the heat.

Quickly fry the tomato and the green pepper in the oil. Add to the sauce, reheat if required, and serve the sauce on the prawns.

This sauce can also be served with pork spareribs or cutlets.

cocktail parties

If you intend to give a large cocktail party, it is not only necessary to have an adequate supply of drinks, but also to arrange your 'house bar'. You may be able to hire a bar, but a table can easily be used, provided the top is protected by a thick pad or is surfaced with formica. Your 'bar' should be easy to clean with a damp cloth.

The following items should be available:

a cocktail shaker of glass or metal, with a good seal
a mixing beaker and a long spoon
a strainer (not made of silver)
a fruit press and a small press for lemon wedges
an ice-bucket and ice-tongs
paper napkins and mats for glasses
drinking straws
tea cloths, various spoons and a measure equalling 1 liqueur glass (2 fl oz)
the right glasses for the various drinks
a wooden board and sharp knives for cutting fruit
a sturdy cotton bag for crushing ice, and a hammer
a bottle of sugar syrup
a bowl of granulated sugar
olives, maraschino cherries, cocktail sticks

As a domestic refrigerator holds only a limited amount of ice, you should try to buy a block in advance. Some fishmongers and frozen food suppliers sell them.

Keep the fruit juices, beer and genevers (Dutch gin) cool in the refrigerator, but never chill liqueurs.

A refrigerated bag, as used on picnics, is also very useful. Do not forget to put ashtrays on the bar: it will save a lot of mess on your floor. As it is very difficult to know your precise requirements beforehand, it is usually a good idea to have a supply of drinks on a 'sale or return' basis. The bottles which are unopened can then be returned to the supplier. It is not a practical proposition to serve all your guests with every kind of drink they may want. So make up a list of what is available and hang it above the bar. Your budget and your own common sense will guide you as to what to include.

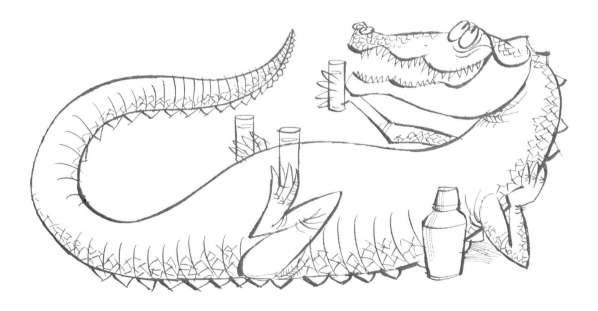

EXTRA DRY MARTINI

1¾ measures dry gin
¼ measure dry white French
 vermouth (Noilly Prat)
 a few drops of Pernod
 ice
 olive

Stir the gin and the vermouth in a mixing beaker with crushed ice and then add a few drops of Pernod. Serve very cold in a cocktail glass with an olive.

GIN & IT

equal parts red vermouth
and gin
ice cubes

Serve well chilled in a whisky glass on the ice.

MANHATTAN SWEET

2 measures bourbon whisky
1 measure red vermouth
2 drops Angostura bitters
 cocktail cherry

Stir the well-chilled drinks together and serve in a cocktail glass. Decorate with a cherry.

MANHATTAN DRY

2 measures Scotch whisky
1 measure dry French
 vermouth
2 drops Angostura bitters
 olive or green cherry

Mix the well-chilled drinks and serve in cocktail glasses. Decorate with an olive or green cherry.

CROCODILE (a recipe by Hugh Jans)

2 measures whisky
½ measure Grand Marnier
½ measure gin
 a dash of tangerine juice
 ice

Shake in the shaker and serve in a whisky glass.

BLOODY MARY

1 measure vodka
 tomato juice to taste
 dash of Worcester sauce

Pour very cold tomato juice into a bell-shaped glass together with the vodka and the Worcester sauce; stir well.

DAIQUIRI

3 parts white rum
1 part lemon juice
3 dashes of sugar syrup
  ice

Shake all the ingredients with the ice in the shaker, and serve very cold.

T.N.T. AMERICAN

1 measure whisky
1 measure Pernod
  ice

Shake with the ice and serve in a whisky glass.

PINK GIN

1 measure gin
3 dashes Angostura

Serve chilled in a small glass.

OLD FASHIONED

1 measure whisky
1 lump of sugar
2 dashes Angostura bitters
2 ice cubes
  lemon peel
$\frac{1}{2}$ slice orange

Stir the ingredients together. Pour them into a tumbler and place the lemon peel and orange slice on top.

WHISKY ON THE ROCKS

whisky
ice cubes

Pour the whisky on the ice cubes in a tumbler.

BLACK BRIDE (a recipe by Hugh Jans)

$\frac{5}{6}$ parts vodka
$\frac{1}{6}$ parts lemon juice
  crushed ice
  black olives

Shake the vodka with the lemon juice and the grated ice, pour in a tumbler and decorate with a black olive.

AMERICAN EGG-NOGG

1 egg
1 teaspoon icing sugar
1 measure port, sherry,
  Calvados or cognac
2 measures single cream
  ice cubes
  nutmeg

Shake all ingredients except the nutmeg vigorously and pour out in a tumbler. Sprinkle nutmeg on top.

MUDDY MAN

1 measure brandy
sugar
nutmeg

Stir the brandy and sugar in a small glass; grate some nutmeg on top.

MARTINI SWEET

2 parts gin
1 part red vermouth
ice
cocktail cherry

Stir the drinks with ice. Serve in cocktail glass with a cherry.

MILKY WAY

$\frac{3}{4}$ measure white crème de menthe
$1\frac{1}{4}$ measures dry gin
crushed ice

Shake in the shaker with the crushed ice. Serve in a cocktail glass.

SARATOGA

2 measures cognac
2 dashes Angostura bitters
1 teaspoon pineapple juice
1 teaspoon Maraschino
crushed ice

Pour the ingredients on the ice; stir well and pour through a sieve into a large glass.

VODKA/ORANGE

3 cubes ice
2 measures vodka
orange juice

Pour the vodka on the ice cubes in a tumbler, and fill up with freshly made orange juice. Stir and enjoy.

SLOE-GIN COCKTAIL

dash Angostura bitters
2 measures sloe gin
crushed ice

Stir the ingredients with the ice in the mixing beaker, and pour through a sieve into the glass.

SPHINX

$1\frac{1}{2}$ measures dry gin
$\frac{1}{4}$ measure sweet vermouth
$\frac{1}{4}$ measure dry vermouth
crushed ice
slice of lemon

Stir the ingredients with the ice in a mixing beaker, and serve with a slice of lemon on top.

LILETH

1 measure green crème de
  menthe
1 measure dry gin
1 measure double cream
  ice cubes

Shake the ingredients with the ice in the shaker. Serve in a cocktail glass.

CUBA LIBRE

1 measure rum
  juice of ½ lemon
  lemon peel
  Coca-cola
  ice

Stir the rum with the juice of the lemon in a tall glass. Place ice cubes in the drink and fill up with ice-cold Coca-cola.

PERNOD

1½ measures Pernod
 2 cubes ice
   ice-cold water

Pour the Pernod over the cubes which have been placed in a tall glass. Serve the ice-cold water separately in a jug.

HIGHBALL

1 measure whisky
  soft drink or ginger ale
  ice
  (lemon peel)

Stir the whisky and the ice in a tall straight glass. Fill up with the soft drink or ginger ale. Stir and serve with the lemon peel on top.

GIN FIZZ

1 measure gin
1 teaspoon icing sugar
  juice of one lemon
  soda water
  ice

Shake the gin with the icing sugar and the lemon juice with the ice. Pour out into a globe-shaped glass and fill up with soda water.

GIN HIGHBALL

1 measure gin
  ginger ale
  peel of 1 lemon

Pour the gin into a tall chilled glass. Fill the glass with ginger ale from the refrigerator. Decorate with thin lemon peel.

SUMMER HOUSE

1½ measures gin
1 measure fresh orange juice
dash of grenadine syrup
soda water
ice cubes

The gin, orange juice and grenadine go into a tall glass with ice cubes. Stir for a moment and fill up with soda water.

APRICOT FIZZ

juice of ¼ orange
juice of ¼ lemon
1 teaspoon icing sugar
1 measure apricot brandy
ice
soda water
1 maraschino cherry

Place fruit juice in the shaker and dissolve the icing sugar in it. Add the apricot brandy and 1 or 2 ice cubes. Close the shaker and shake vigorously. Pour into a tall glass and fill up with chilled soda water. Serve with a cherry and 2 straws.

SLOE GIN SODA

1½ measures sloe gin
3 ice cubes
soda water
1 slice of lemon

Stir the sloe gin with 3 ice cubes in the mixing beaker. Add soda water and a slice of lemon and pour into a long drink glass.

CRÈME DE MENTHE SODA

1 measure crème de menthe
2 ice cubes
soda water

Combine crème de menthe with ice cubes in a long drink glass. Fill up with soda water.

RUM COOLER

juice of ¼ lemon
1 measure pineapple syrup
1 measure rum
crushed ice
any soft drink

Stir the lemon, pineapple syrup and rum together in a large glass with a stem. Half-fill the glass with crushed ice, pour in a soft drink and place 2 straws in it.

ORANGE COLLINS

juice of 1 orange
2 lumps of sugar
dash of Angostura bitters
2 teaspoons water
2 measures gin
5 ice cubes
soda water

Rub the two lumps of sugar over the orange peel until they have well absorbed the orange flavour. Place them in a long drink glass with a dash of Angostura bitters and 2 teaspoons water, the gin and the juice of an orange. Add 5 cubes of ice and stir until the glass is 'steamed' up. Fill up with soda water. Place orange slice on the edge of the glass.

HORSE'S TAIL

the entire peel of a lemon
2 ice cubes
a few drops of Angostura bitters
ginger ale

Peel the lemon in such a way that a long spiral of peel results. Place this spiral in a tumbler and hang the end over the edge (forming the tail). Add 2 ice cubes. Sprinkle a few drops of Angostura bitters on top and fill the tumbler with ginger ale.

MA COLLINS

juice of 1 lemon
icing sugar to taste
4 ice cubes
soda water

While the other guests are drinking Tom and John Collinses (for the former one use gin and for the latter old Dutch gin), prepare Ma Collins in the same way but without alcohol. From the outside they look the same.

ORANGE COCKTAIL

6 measures orange juice
1 egg
4 teaspoons granulated sugar

Use the mixer for this. Mix the egg with the sugar and the well-chilled orange juice until the mixture froths up. Serve in a well-chilled large wine glass.

HONOLULU

1½ measures orange juice
1½ measures pineapple juice
dash of lemon juice
2 dashes grenadine syrup
crushed ice

Shake all the ingredients in the shaker with the crushed ice and pour through a strainer into a large chilled glass.

TOMATO COCKTAIL

3 measures tomato juice
dash lemon juice
pinch salt
pinch pepper
pinch celery salt
a little sugar
½ teaspoon Worcester sauce
ice cube

Stir all the ingredients with the ice cube in the mixing beaker. Pour into a large glass.

simply wine and cheese

History has never made clear who invented the combination of wine and cheese. It must have been a gastronomic genius. Possibly he or she was Persian. After all, Persia is the country of origin of many of the arts of living. It was the birthplace of many of our musical instruments, the first home of many of our fruits and flowers, and also, possibly, of wine and cheese.

We consider it obvious to combine wine and cheese, yet somebody must have been the first to think of it. Wine and cheese form a cosmos of heaven and earth: good cheese is a product of the earth, fertile soil, the smell and warmth of animals inside the protective stable. Wine, on the other hand, is spiritual, sublimated sunshine; wine lifts up the spirit and removes our earthly worries. In this way wine and cheese complement each other in complete harmony, with bread as the link between them. 'A triple blessing as old as the world', is a well-known description of bread, wine and cheese.

Wine and cheese, then, belong together as the dew and the rose, as the wind and the sea. In France they call it a 'bon mariage'; and the refined art of combining various wines and cheeses is truly French.

There are few countries with so many possibilities. France makes nearly four hundred different cheeses. General de Gaulle is said to have declared that a country with so many different cheeses was impossible to govern! But besides the cheeses, there are several thousands of different wines. One would require many lives to try out all the possible combinations. However, the knowledge that we shall never know all that can be achieved should not discourage us; let us try and see how far we can get.

Wine-and-cheese parties can develop their own specific character. They can become either homely intimate

evenings with our friends, some bottles of wine and a cheese board, or cheerful occasions for a crowd or club. Nothing, oddly enough, could be more remote from the French way of using either.

In France cheese is still eaten almost exclusively as part of a meal, after the meat course and before the sweet, in order to enjoy at leisure the red wine of the main course. The 'wine-and-cheese party', although using French wines and cheeses, is not known in France at all.

Wine-and-cheese parties among friends demand soft candlelight and music. The wine and cheese we give our intimates should be too good to be consumed thoughtlessly. They should not be a backcloth to the party; they should be its centrepiece. They demand attention and the right atmosphere.

The surroundings are of the utmost importance for this kind of wine-and-cheese evening. Arrange your easy chairs round a low table. Take special care that there is enough room for the candles — after all, the colour of the wine improves greatly in the soft candlelight — glasses, cheese board, bread basket, butter dishes, napkins, possibly small plates and knives, all should be ready. One corner of the room can be lit by an old-fashioned paraffin light — but it must be one which does not smell at all; otherwise the exquisite bouquet of the wine will be spoilt. Collect all your candle-holders and add some decorative bottles. The table can be set informally — for instance with a gay linen cloth; place on it the wine glasses, cheese, some grapes, and your choice of breads.

Arrange the various kinds of bread in the bread basket. Have French loaves, of course, which you can make warm and crisp by placing them for a short while in a hot oven just before use, rye bread, wholemeal bread, have some crackers too. For people who like to eat bread with butter, put out butter dishes and knives. In order to make things easy for your guests, use little individual butter-pots, smooth the butter on the top and draw a pattern on it. Arrange the various cheeses on the board and place cheese knives for each at the side. Instead of the board, you may like to use the decorative board mats which one usually sees as table mats. If you are the lucky possessor of a marble slab this is your opportunity to make full use of it. Whatever you do to present your cheese, never place it on paper or linen napkins; in the heat of the room the cheese may melt. But each guest must be provided with a napkin, and a linen one is much more attractive than a paper one. If the company is small and informal, you may be able to manage without plates: the bread is broken and the cheese knives are used to put some cheese on top. However, it is better to provide each guest with a small plate and knife if you can.

Make the cheese board attractive with some red radish rosettes, small bunches of white and black grapes, some nuts and stuffed olives. In a narrow tall glass, place some celery sticks. Celery goes well with cheese, and together with red wine it forms an excellent combination.

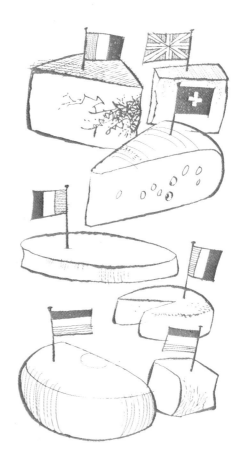

the wine

All the wine cellars of Europe are at your disposal. For any wine-and-cheese party you can choose as you like, according to your budget, your palate, the taste of your friends, or the crowd you invite. You can choose a simple village wine, or an elegant and delicately balanced red Bordeaux, a gay rose, or a dark and mysterious Burgundy, a fresh, sparkling Moselle or a spicy Château Neuf du Pape. Wine is not as difficult to choose as it is often reputed to be. It does not require much more attention than other drinks — coffee, tea, beer and fruit juices also need to be at the right temperature to be at their best; beer and spirits should be served in the appropriate glasses — wine is so often blamed for things which are considered obvious in other drinks!

The simpler the wine, the less it demands. But never buy the wine at the last possible moment, even if it is a very modest variety. Village, a light rose, or a cheap white wine can be bought an hour or two beforehand, if necessary. But if you wish to serve a better wine it is wise to buy it at least a week before the event. Quality wines require time to adjust, settle and become accustomed to the temperature of your room.

If you are expecting guests who have little experience in the enjoyment of wine do not present them with a very expensive wine, but do give them a reasonably good one. They will only learn to like wine if you give them a chance to respect it. Wine is an acquired taste. Remember, however, that no one needs to be ashamed about a humble wine, provided the wine is good of its kind. A person who calls himself a wine expert and who looks down on a village wine, is usually no expert, but a wine snob.

If on a special evening you want to enjoy a superb wine, then invite a few guests who you know will appreciate it and who will share your enjoyment and enthusiasm. If ever the company of friends is a double pleasure, it is with a really fine bottle of wine.

White and rose wines are served cool, but never ice cold. Ice-cold wine loses the bouquet, which is one of its essential features. Sweet white wines, sparkling wines and rose wines need be slightly chilled, as a rule.

Red wines should be served at room temperature. Put the bottle out in the morning in a normally heated room, and the wine will be just at its right temperature at night. Open the bottle at least an hour before serving it, to give it a chance to 'breathe'. This process lets it develop its possibilities to the full. Never try to bring a red wine quickly at the required temperature by placing it near a stove, or even worse, placing it in a container of hot water. Such barbaric treatment will turn any red wine and certainly a red Bordeaux hard and acid-tasting. If you forget to place the wine in the right room in time or if the idea for a wine evening is a sudden one, serve a fresh young Beaujolais, which can be served cool, or a white or rose wine.

Always serve wine in a sparklingly clean glass which is only filled half full. Wine requires space. Space to move, space to develop its attractions of aroma and bouquet! In a glass filled to the brim, it has no room to give of its best. Even the most beautiful, rich wine can seem lean and 'flat' if served in too small a glass, where there is no room for movement. The ideal wine glass has a slightly inward bent brim, in order to retain all the subtlety of the bouquet until the moment of your first encounter with it, and also all the flavour your palate should enjoy.

the cheese

Although wine should be bought in advance of being drunk, cheese is best bought at the last moment. When buying wine, you study the label, but cheese must be more closely inspected. Most good grocers will let you taste it before you buy too. The appearance of English and some other cheeses is no doubt well known to you, but there are some foreign varieties which are difficult to assess. In some of these foreign cheeses, the correct degree of ripeness is extremely important. Soft cheeses, such as Brie, Munster or Camembert, must be just ripe.

If they are too young, the aroma has not yet developed: when too old both smell and taste become unpleasant and sharp. The ripeness can be tested by slightly pressing the centre of the cheese. The cheese should feel soft. If the cheese is cut, then the inside should be yellow and moist but not sloppy. If at all possible, do not buy these cheeses in small sections wrapped in silver paper, but whole in a chip box, or fresh from the mat.

The white rind of cheeses such as Camembert can easily be eaten (provided the cheese is not too mature). Many devotees even think that a Camembert without its rind is like an egg without salt. Cheese varieties with an orangey rind, such as Dutch Kernhem and French Port Salut, should always be eaten without their rind. Blue veined cheeses, such as Dutch Bluefort, Danish Blue, French Roquefort and Italian Gorgonzola must be firm in consistency with some blue-green veins and the colour of the cheese itself should be creamy white and definitely not grey or yellow: if it is the cheese is too old.

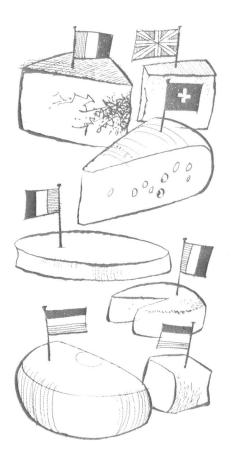

the actual combining

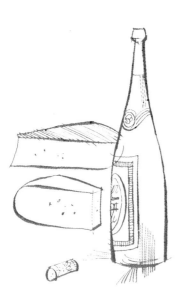

Even though wine and cheese form a delightful combination, there are so many wines and cheeses that a careless combination can be 'just wrong'. In judging what to combine, the most important opinion is your own: by trial and error, you will discover certain combinations which suit your taste, even though they may not be the generally accepted ones. Your own taste is more important than the rules and regulations of a booklet. This is why you should provide at least two varieties of cheeses for any cheese-and-wine party; everyone should have the opportunity to experiment. In any case, no wine or cheese tastes quite the same each time, nor will your own mood and taste be the same. Even though you may have been enchanted by a particular combination once, you may be disillusioned the next time. On the other hand a combination may have new charms at a second trial.

That is the most delightful aspect of a wine-and-cheese party. It is always different, and always surprising.

There are, however, certain rules which must be observed. One of the most important ones is that wine and cheese must complement one another. The one should never dominate the other. This is why a soft and pleasant cheese is eaten with a soft and pleasant wine, whereas the full-bodied heavy wines should be accompanied by a savoury, even sharp cheese. Young and fruity wines can 'take' a somewhat sour cheese, and wines on the sweeter side prefer a cheese with a broad, rich and creamy flavour. Remember that in the combination of wine and cheese, the wine plays the most important part. Have the courage to experiment. Give your guests a surprise with an unusual cheese. Leave them to try its taste and try again. The exchange of special 'finds' can make an evening an adventure. In a large company, and certainly when you serve two wines, six or eight cheese varieties are not too many. And when you have crisp French bread, the wine at the correct temperature, the cheese in its prime and when the candle light glimmers on the polished glasses, then you have done everything possible to guarantee a perfect evening — the wine will do the rest to gladden the heart of men.

ideas for the combination of wine and cheese

With white wines, such as Moselle wine and white Burgundy, serve:
soft cheeses such as Gouda or Edam, Port Salut, Saint Paulin. Also Swiss cheeses such as Gruyère and Emmenthaler. As a special cheese: Leyden.

With semi-sweet wines, such as many Loire wines and white Bordeaux serve:
fresh cheese, such as Gervais; Swiss cheeses such as Emmenthaler and Gruyère.

With rose wines serve:
goat's milk cheeses, Tome de raisins.

With light, young, red wines, such as fresh Beaujolais or Chianti serve:
goat's milk cheese, young Edam, Pont L'Eveque, Kernhem, Brie. With Chianti, also try Bel Paese and Gorgonzola.

With elegant, delicate red wines, serve:
young natural Gouda, Brie, Saint Marcellin, Reblochon.

With fuller red wines, serve:
mature Gouda, Brie, Roquefort (and other French blue cheeses, such as Bresse Bleu), Camembert and Tilsiter.

With heavy red wines, such as Saint Emilion, Côte de Nuits, serve:
mature Gouda, mature Edam, Roquefort, and other French blue cheeses or Camembert.

With spicy red wines, such as Côtes du Rhône, serve:
mature Gouda or Edam, Roquefort and other blue cheeses, or Cantal.

With port, serve:
mature Gouda, Dolcelatte, Stilton.

fondues – for informal parties

There are two kinds of fondue, which are completely different: the cheese fondue (which is the real fondue) and the meat fondue (which is not a fondue at all). The word fondue means 'melted' and the word certainly applies to the cheese fondue, which consists of wine and melted cheese. But meat fondues consist of pieces of meat fried in very hot fat. The meat fondue – which originated in the Far East – gets its name from the fact that it is eaten in the same style as the cheese fondue: everyone sits around a heated pan in which he dips his own bite-sized pieces of food.

A fondue party is an excellent way for a hostess to entertain friends and family for a meal without too much trouble.

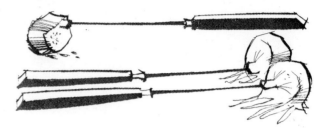

cheese fondue

The cheese fondue is a Swiss invention. It is a very old dish, and a famous one, which was described in the old, great standard work of gastronomy 'La Physiologie du Gout' by Brillat-Savarin, although his was a somewhat different fondue from the one we know, more like an omelet with cheese than a proper fondue.

What we consider to be a 'correct' cheese fondue — cheese melted in wine — is a speciality from the Neuchâtel district and is said to have been invented by the wife of a wine farmer. (Neuchâtel has many excellent vineyards, where a fresh, gay sparkling wine is produced.) During harvest time the entire family of the wine farmer was so busy with grape-picking, that there was little time left for his wife to cook. Yet the reapers always had an enormous appetite. Her solution was ingenious: when they returned home at night tired from a heavy day's work, the wine of the previous harvest was placed on the fire and cheese was added to it; within a quarter of an hour, the family was gathered around a most nourishing meal.

CHEESE FONDUE FROM NEUCHÂTEL

8 oz Emmenthaler cheese
8 oz Gruyère cheese
¾ pint dry white wine
2 cloves garlic, cut in half
1 small glass kirsch
1 teaspoon cornflour
  pepper
  nutmeg

For a cheese fondue you need a 'caquelon', a flat saucepan usually made of copper or earthenware. Cheese fondue should not be made in an aluminium pan, as the bottom becomes far too hot. Rub the caquelon with the cut garlic. Grate the cheese or cut it into very thin strips and place them on the bottom of the caquelon, pour the wine on top and place the pan on the methylated-spirit heater. Stir with a wooden spoon, always describing the figure 8 in the same direction. Slowly but surely the substance will thicken and become creamy. Mix the cornflour with the kirsch; this kirsch is necessary to make the fondue digestible; it can be bought in miniature bottles. Stir this into the fondue. Finally, dust liberally with freshly-ground pepper and season the fondue with a little nutmeg.

On your central table, place baskets filled with hunks of bread. Every guest takes one and cuts it into small cubes. He sticks a cube of bread (preferably with the crust still on it) on a long fondue fork, dips this in the bubbling fondue, and eats the fondue straight from the pan. If he loses his piece of bread in the fondue, he has to give his hostess a bottle of wine or invite the company for the next party.

It is often said that a white wine must be served with a fondue. This is not so. If one eats fondue around Neuchâtel, in the homes of the wine farmers, wine is in fact never served with it. Indeed a cold white wine does not really go well with a fondue. The white wine is served beforehand, as an apéritif.

A Swiss white wine is most suitable. One of the best Swiss wines is the Fendant, from Valais. It is an excellent dry and light white wine, which is always poured out from the bottle held high above the glass, so that the wine enters the glass slightly foaming. The wine must have air, say the Swiss, and they should know. The Fendant thus obtains its tingling freshness which recalls the sparkling mountain air near the snowfields.

This wine should be chilled although only slightly. In Switzerland, it is served in small-sized water-glasses. Try to find these special glasses; they are pleasant and go well with the informal fondue table setting.

The best drink to serve with the fondue itself is fresh strong tea.

After a fondue you should serve a light dessert such as meringue, a compote of fruit or a fruit salad; and, finally, strong hot coffee, preferably with a glass of kirsch or cognac.

There are many variations on this basic recipe for cheese fondue.

FONDUE WITH HERBS

Cut fresh garden herbs, such as chives, chervil, parsley, tarragon and lemon thyme; chop the herbs and stir them into the fondue when it is finished.

MUSHROOM FONDUE

Pale-coloured types of mushrooms should be used; for example, button mushrooms (which should be very finely chopped and added together with the wine).

HAM FONDUE

At the last minute, add some very finely chopped raw or boiled ham and some parsley to the fondue.

TOMATO FONDUE

Stir 1 tablespoon tomato purée into $\frac{1}{2}$ pint wine. Add some herbs, such as finely cut chives and very finely grated shallot.

BEER FONDUE

This is an English invention, or so they say abroad, and therefore an English cheese such as Cheddar, Cheshire or Lancashire should be used instead of a Swiss cheese. Use a light beer instead of white wine and add a pinch of dry mustard. For the rest, proceed as with the classic cheese fondue. If you wish, the French loaf can be replaced by brown bread or wholemeal bread as the rough texture is in many ways better suited to the beer flavour than the more neutral white bread.

As you come to the end of a fondue, you will find a thin brown crust on the bottom of the caquelon. This is considered the best part of the fondue and should be shared equally by all the participants.

meat fondues

The classic meat fondue is a 'Fondue Bourguignonne'. From this, you may assume that it originated in Burgundy. Don't you believe it! No true Burgundian would dream of frying small pieces of meat in fat and eating fancy sauces with it. The traditional Burgundian cuisine is one of classical sauces which have been reduced for hours with wine and herbs, of complicated meat dishes, the preparation of which may commence 24 hours beforehand, and of slowly simmered dishes with infinite personal variations. The origin of 'Fondue Bourguignonne' is not Burgundy; it is not even Switzerland, but right on the other side of the globe in the Far East. In Japan, a geisha, kneeling beside your table, fries tit-bits of meat, fish or vegetables in hot oil, and you have an array of bowls in front of you containing superb sauces and pickles to dip them in. A similar dish comes from Indonesia. By various routes, this way of preparing food has ended up in Switzerland. It has come to be called 'a fondue' because it calls, like a cheese fondue, for a pan set over a flame on the table.

The origin of the word 'Bourguignonne' remains a riddle. It is sometimes said that it has been added because red Burgundy tastes so well with the fried meat. But this is not really so; a red Burgundy is not the ideal wine to serve with a 'Fondue Bourguignonne'. There are other wines which are far better suited to it.

FONDUE BOURGUIGNONNE

The recipe for Fondue Bourguignonne is simple. Heat oil or fat in a copper fondue pan until it is very hot; then place the pan over a methylated-spirit heater on the table. Stick pieces of tender, lean meat on a long fondue fork, dip them into the hot oil, fry until golden-brown and eat the meat with the various sauces which should be set ready in small bowls on the table.

Most recipes stipulate olive oil. But although olive oil is essential for some dishes, it is in fact better to use sunflower oil for a 'fondue Bourguignonne'. It produces less smoke, and is more neutral. A good vegetable fat is also suitable. But never use butter; it does not reach a high enough temperature and it burns quickly.

The meat most often recommended for a fondue is fillet of beef. But real fillet of beef has become exorbitantly expensive and it is not really necessary to use it. Thick juicy sirloin, rump or topside can be used equally well.

The meat should not be seasoned beforehand, as salt draws the juices out of the meat, and makes the outside difficult to fry. Take care that the fat or oil remains very hot; you can even take the pan back to the kitchen halfway through the party, to reheat it. If the fat is too cool, the meat will have an unpleasant taste, and be greasy.

The most exciting part of the fondue is the many different sauces into which the meat is dipped. You can use your imagination, to enjoy creating them, since anything goes! One good basis is a salad cream, or mayonnaise, which is whipped lighter with cream and egg white. Various savoury flavourings can then be added. Some suggestions follow but they are not the whole story; there are scores more which are known to be equally successful, and you can add your own inventions.

To make the basic sauce, put $\frac{1}{2}$ pint light salad cream or mayonnaise into a basin. Whip 1 egg white and a pinch of salt in a separate small basin until very stiff. In a third basin, whip $\frac{1}{4}$ pint double cream until semi-stiff. Gradually trickle in $\frac{1}{8}$ pint milk or single cream while continuing to whip. Keep on whipping until the cream is almost as stiff as the egg white. Very gently, fold the egg white into it. Then fold the salad cream or mayonnaise in likewise. As variations, stir the following into $\frac{1}{2}$ pint of the basic sauce and adjust the quantities to suit your own taste.

1 or 2 finely cut fresh garden herbs such as chives, parsley, chervil, shallot, tarragon, lemon thyme, marjoram;

2 tablespoons grated apple, a few drops of cognac;

2 tablespoons mixed finely cut apple and onion, fried gently for a few moments with a pinch of curry powder;

2 teaspoons finely chopped onion and garlic, mixed with a pinch of chilli sauce.

$\frac{1}{2}$ teaspoon anchovy paste and 2 tablespoons tomato purée or ketchup;

2 teaspoons ground almonds, 1 dash of sherry, 1 teaspoon finely chopped green olives;

2 teaspoons finely chopped black olives and a squeezed $\frac{1}{2}$ clove garlic;

1 tablespoon grated onion, a pinch of dry mustard, some finely chopped, pipped grapes

2 teaspoons grated lemon peel, 1 teaspoon capers, and 1 tablespoon tomato purée;

2 teaspoons grated orange peel, a dash of vermouth, and some drops of orange juice;

2 teaspoons finely chopped ginger and ginger syrup, mixed.

Use 3 or 4 of these cold sauces, and at least 1 hot spicy sauce such as a classic Piquant Sauce.

Place the sauces in bowls on the table. Add a basket containing large pieces of French bread, and complete the course with pleasant side dishes, such as gherkins and onions, salted almonds, black and green olives, chutney, red chillis and mixed pickles. Make a careful selection which complements your chosen sauces. You will also need to supply your guests with napkins, glasses, and a second fork each. One does not eat the meat with the same fork which one has used for frying. It will be much too hot. If you have guests who are enjoying their first 'fondue meal' you must warn them that the meat is very hot too, when it comes out of the boiling fat.

You can serve a wine with a meat fondue but never waste a delicate, old or expensive one. The spicy, savoury, slightly sweet or sour sauces are far too pronounced for such wines. The best wine to serve with a fondue is a fresh, young, Beaujolais or a Côtes du Rhône.

After the fondue, serve a mature semi-hard cheese to finish off the wine, and then, fresh fruit. Follow it with strong coffee, and a glass of cognac for those who like it.

JAPANESE FONDUE (SUKIYAKI)

If you wish to ring the changes on your meat fondue, why not return to the country of origin, Japan, and invite your guests to a Western sukiyaki party?

In the centre of the table place the same small pan with hot oil on its heater as for the Fondue Bourguignonne. But this time do not only serve meat; add small pieces of vegetable, such as strips of cucumber, cauliflower rosettes, whole baby onions, strips of celeriac, bamboo shoots, tinned artichoke hearts and strips of red or greenbell pepper. All these are fried in the hot oil or fat.

Each guest has a small bowl in front of him containing a raw yolk of egg mixed with a little soy sauce. We Europeans sometimes put out dishes of pickles, chutney and so on too, but this is not authentic; you can serve the famous Japanese rice vermicelli in small bowls if you can get hold of it.

If you wish to eat sukiyaki in the true Japanese style too, do not use forks to cook and eat with. Hold your vegetables and meat tit-bits with chopsticks to dip them in the hot oil and then eat them. However, this requires a good deal of skill, and if you fear to lose them it may be a better idea to use the forks.

¼ pint water
2 tablespoons sherry
pinch of ground ginger
pinch of sugar
dash of soy sauce

CHINESE FONDUE

If you want to avoid having a lingering oily smoke in your room, you may like to try a Chinese fondue. In this dish, the meat and the pieces of vegetables are not fried in fat but boiled in a broth. Have a light broth or bouillon flavoured with a variety of herbs and strained.

Bring it almost to the boil and keep it just at simmering point on the methylated-spirit burner. You can use your cheese fondue caquelon for this. In the broth you cook bite-sized pieces of meat, small strips of raw chicken, cauliflower rosettes, button mushrooms and small pieces of celeriac for a short time. As a sauce use the raw egg mixed with soy sauce above or, if you wish, a Piquant sauce or spicy chutney.

When all the meat and vegetables have been eaten, your broth will be really full flavoured. Add a dash of sherry and serve it in small bowls or cups.

The correct wine to drink with a Chinese or Japanese fondue is saké. This is rice wine which is served (often warm) in small porcelain cups. As saké is difficult to get, you can try using a light dry sherry instead; it is not dissimilar in taste.

After this meal, do not serve coffee but one of the aromatic Chinese teas in small cups.

CHOCOLATE FONDUE

Sweet fondues are a modern, Western idea. The most popular of these innovations on the fondue scene is the chocolate fondue.

Break bars of bitter chocolate into small pieces, and put into the caquelon of your cheese fondue set with 1 tablespoon water to 1 oz chocolate. Melt gently. Then add a little strong black coffee, make sure that the chocolate is hot but *not* boiling, and add a dash or two of double cream and 1–2 tablespoons of rum or an orange-flavoured liqueur. See that the fondue does not reach the boil after this. On the table round the caquelon, place bowls containing cubes of firm plain cake, pieces of banana, pear, pineapple and some skinned sections of orange. The guests spear these on fondue forks and dip them into the liquid chocolate.

A chocolate fondue makes a delicious follow-up to a main course of roast or casseroled chicken or veal, rice or *pasta*. But never, never follow a main course fondue with a sweet fondue.

a running buffet

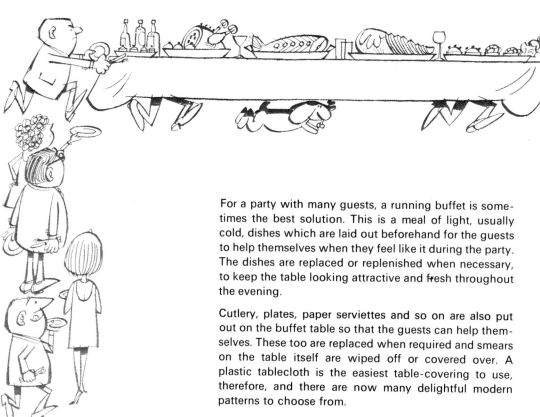

For a party with many guests, a running buffet is sometimes the best solution. This is a meal of light, usually cold, dishes which are laid out beforehand for the guests to help themselves when they feel like it during the party. The dishes are replaced or replenished when necessary, to keep the table looking attractive and fresh throughout the evening.

Cutlery, plates, paper serviettes and so on are also put out on the buffet table so that the guests can help themselves. These too are replaced when required and smears on the table itself are wiped off or covered over. A plastic tablecloth is the easiest table-covering to use, therefore, and there are now many delightful modern patterns to choose from.

Tell your guests beforehand what to expect, especially if you lay the buffet in a separate room from where the drinks are being served. Otherwise, they may wait for you to announce a set meal and go hungry. Alternatively, put a poster on the supper-room door; but in this case you run the risk of shy guests being reluctant to take the initiative and help themselves until the room is already crowded. Crowding is just what you want to avoid.

Platters of cold fish, game or sliced meats, cold sliced or jointed poultry with an interesting sauce, a cheese board and French bread are usually enough. Do not make too many separate dishes as you then risk having a wide variety of leftovers. But do take care to see that the dishes' main colours are different, and try to create a colour scheme for your table decoration which tones in with them.

The art of planning a running buffet is to time the first drinks so that the assault on the sideboard begins while the rapid drinkers are still interested in food. In other words, do not start the party too early; nor yet so late that your guests have eaten a lot of snacks beforehand.

If your buffet and drinks are in the same room, it will encourage a continuous movement between the food and drink. But if not, have scattered about the room some tasty tit-bits and snacks in shallow dishes or on wooden trays. Here are a few suggestions:

EGG BUTTER ROUNDS

Make a paste of mashed hard-boiled egg yolks and softened butter, season it with salt, finely chopped mixed herbs, freshly ground black pepper and a pinch of nutmeg. Spread this mixture on rounds of bread which have been cut from white sliced bread.

BLUE CHEESE SPREAD

Make a spread of any good blue cheese mixed with butter, a little sherry, paprika and cayenne pepper; cover small square pieces of toast with it.

SPICED CRAB SNACKS

Cover small, crisp biscuits with a mixture of mashed crab (from a tin), spiced with some ground cumin, curry powder and a little garlic salt.

STUFFED CUCUMBER SLICES

Peel two large cucumbers and remove the end pieces. Cut them into sections about 3 inches long. Remove the centres to make cucumber tubes with walls approximately $\frac{1}{2}$ inch thick. Steep them in water with 1 tablespoon salt for twenty minutes. Make a filling of 1 cup crabmeat, 4 mashed hard-boiled egg yolks, 2 tablespoons mayonnaise and a little salt and pepper. Remove the hollow pieces of cucumber from the water and dry them well. Fill them with the crab mixture and leave in the refrigerator for 1 hour, then cut them into thick slices.

HERRING TOASTIES

Remove the bones from 4 small smoked herrings, mash the flesh with 4 tablespoons double cream and 2 tablespoons olive oil until thoroughly blended. Season to taste with lemon juice, salt and pepper. Spread small rounds of buttered toast with the mixture and sprinkle some finely chopped radish or parsley on top.

For the larger dishes on the buffet itself, choose from among the following:

CHICKEN LIVER PÂTÉ

2 finely chopped
  onions
2 cloves of garlic,
  squeezed
2 oz butter
1 lb 2 oz chicken livers
3 sprigs parsley
1 pinch thyme
2 bay leaves
  salt
  black pepper
1 tablespoon cognac

Fry the onions and garlic in the butter until soft but not brown. Chop the chicken livers and add them; add the herbs too, and leave to simmer for 5 minutes, allow to cool, then chop as finely as possible. Add the butter from the pan and the cognac. For a firm pâté mix in 1–2 tablespoons powdered gelatine dissolved in 2 tablespoons water and some lemon juice or port.

Fill a pâté dish with the mixture and press it well down. Leave to firm up in the refrigerator.

LIVER PÂTÉ WITH OLIVES

1 lb 10 oz pig's liver
1 lb 1½ oz fat pork
¾ pt milk
1 3-oz glass dry sherry
4 oz flour
2 tablespoons ground allspice
  salt
  pepper
8 chopped black olives
4 oz butter, melted

Chop the liver and the pork finely. Mix together. Add the milk and sherry, then the flour, allspice, salt, pepper, the finely chopped olives and the melted butter.

Put the mixture into a buttered metal baking tin. Place it in a pan of cold water. Cover the baking tin with aluminium foil and place everything for one hour in the oven heated to 180°C, 350°F, Gas Mark 4. Remove the tin from the oven and leave to cool.

SALMON PÂTÉ

1 large can salmon (1 lb
  1½ oz)
3 tablespoons dry sherry
1 lb 1½ oz whiting
2 oz freshly made white
  breadcrumbs
1 oz butter, melted
1 teaspoon salt
¼ teaspoon pepper
  pinch cayenne pepper
  pinch of ground fennel
  juice of 1 lemon
1 egg yolk

Remove the bones from the salmon and leave to marinate in the sherry for 2–3 hours, turning the salmon over occasionally. Clean and fillet the whiting, if necessary. Chop, together with the salmon and mix the two well. Add the breadcrumbs, butter, salt, pepper, cayenne pepper, fennel, lemon juice and yolk of egg. Blend everything together thoroughly, until a smooth paste. Transfer this to a buttered baking tin. Press the pâté down well into the tin. Cover with aluminium foil and bake for 1 hour in a moderate oven, heated to 180°C, 350°F, Gas Mark 4. Remove the tin from the oven, place a wooden board with something heavy on it on top of the pâté and leave overnight in a cool place. Next morning turn the pâté out on to a flat dish and decorate with lettuce leaves, slices of tomato and chopped parsley.

SALMON BREAD IN ASPIC

1 tablespoon powdered
  gelatine
$\frac{1}{6}$ pint cold water
  juice of $\frac{1}{2}$ lemon
1 lb 1$\frac{1}{2}$ oz canned red salmon
8 oz soft Gervais or cottage
  cheese
1 teacup mayonnaise
$\frac{1}{2}$ green pepper
$\frac{1}{2}$ onion, finely chopped
2 tablespoons finely chopped
  chives or parsley
1 teaspoon salt
  pinch of cayenne pepper
$\frac{1}{4}$ cucumber, sliced

Sprinkle the gelatine on the cold water in the pan and leave it for 5 minutes. Then warm it slowly over a low heat, and stir until the gelatine has melted. Do not let it come to the boil. Remove from the heat and stir in the lemon juice. Leave to cool until semi-set. Remove the bones from the salmon and mix with the cheese and mayonnaise. Add the finely chopped green pepper, the onion, and the chives or parsley. Mix well.

Pour 2–3 tablespoons of the lemon-juice jelly into a baking tin which has been wetted with cold water and place a neat row of overlapping cucumber slices on top. Put the mould into the refrigerator until the contents have set firmly. In the meantime, mix the remainder of the jelly with the salmon mixture. Spoon into the mould. Place in the refrigerator to set fully. Turn the set salmon loaf on to a flat dish and decorate with the remaining cucumber slices.

CRAB TOMATOES

8 tomatoes
8 oz canned crabmeat
2 finely chopped hard-boiled
  eggs
3 tablespoons Béchamel
  sauce
1 tablespoon double cream,
  whipped half-stiff

Dip the tomatoes in boiling water and skin them. Cut off the tops for lids and carefully spoon out the insides. Wrap the fruit shells loosely in aluminium foil and place them in the refrigerator. Mash the crabmeat finely and mix with the finely chopped eggs. Blend with the Béchamel sauce and then fold in the cream. Fill the tomato shells and place the lids on top. Serve on rounds of toast.

EGGS STUFFED WITH SHRIMPS

4 hard-boiled eggs
5 oz freshly peeled shrimps
$\frac{1}{2}$ pint condensed cream of
  celery soup
$\frac{1}{2}$ teaspoon ground dried
  tarragon

Shell the hard-boiled eggs and cut them lengthwise. Remove the yolks.

Chop the shrimps coarsely and stir them into the celery soup without thinning it. Add the finely ground dried tarragon. Fill the egg halves with this shrimp ragoût and sprinkle some sieved yolk of egg on top.

ORANGES STUFFED WITH SARDINES

6 medium-sized oranges
1 lemon
1 3⅓-oz tin sardines
5 oz butter
  mustard
  paprika
  black pepper
1 egg white, stiffly whipped
  ground marjoram
12 fresh mint leaves

Cut the oranges into halves and remove the flesh. Scrape away as much of the pith as possible. Remove the pips from the orange pulp.

Make the sardines, butter and mustard into a firm paste and season with paprika and pepper. Fold in as much of the orange pulp and juice, lemon juice and egg white as suits your taste. Season the mixture with marjoram and fill the orange halves.

Leave the oranges to firm up in the refrigerator, and decorate them with the mint leaves before serving.

COLD CHICKEN WITH CRAB SAUCE

1 3½–4 lb roasting chicken
  salt and pepper
1 onion
1 small leek
4 oz butter
1½ gills mayonnaise
⅛ pint single cream
¼ teaspoon ground celery
  seeds or ½ teaspoon
  finely chopped green
  celery
  pepper
  squeeze of garlic
4–5 oz tinned crab

Season the inside and outside of the chicken with salt and pepper and place an onion and a small leek inside it. Roast in a slow oven basting the chicken frequently. Remove the chicken from the oven when cooked. Skin it and when it is cool remove the bones. Cut the meat into equal-sized slices and arrange them, overlapping, on a platter. Mix the remaining ingredients to make a sauce, and spoon over the chicken.

TONGUE IN BROWN VELVET

2 smoked calves' tongues,
  about 1 lb each
  onion, carrot, leek, parsley,
  clove, bay leaf, mace and
  pepper
2 ½-pint tins condensed oxtail
  or brown vegetable soup
2 tablespoons single cream
1 wine glass Madeira
2 tablespoons raisins

Soak the tongues overnight. Next day, remove them from the water and bring them to the boil in fresh water with the onion, cloves, carrot, leek, parsley, bay leaf, mace and pepper. Simmer for 1½ hours or until tender. If you can stick a fork easily into the thickest part, the tongues are ready.

Remove the tongues from the stock, leave them to cool a little and then skin them. (Save the stock; it will make an excellent soup afterwards.) Cut the tongues into equal-sized slices about ¼ inch thick and arrange in overlapping layers on a serving dish. Stir the cream and Madeira into the soup, without thinning it. Add the raisins. Heat the soup slowly until almost on the boil, then leave to cool. The soup should be the consistency of a clinging sauce. (Garlic can be added for those who like it.) Spoon the sauce over the tongue shortly before serving.

CHICKEN WITH MUSHROOM SAUCE

1¾ lb boned chicken meat
½ pint of condensed cream of
 mushroom soup
1 tablespoon chopped onion,
 lightly fried
1 tablespoon chopped
 parsley
½ teaspoon poultry
 seasoning
¾ teaspoon salt

Arrange the meat in an attractive pattern on a decorative platter. Make a sauce of the condensed soup by adding the fried onion and parsley, poultry seasoning and salt. Stir and bring slowly to the boil over a low heat. Continue stirring until the sauce is well reduced. Leave to cool then spoon over the chicken slices on the platter. If necessary, chill for a short while before serving.

DOVER SOLE WITH SHRIMP SAUCE AND GRAPES

3 medium-sized soles
 ground tarragon
 fish heads and bones
1 onion, chopped
1 carrot, chopped
1 leek, sliced
½ bay leaf
 mace
 pepper and salt
8 tablespoons butter
4 finely chopped shallots
 salt and pepper
¼ pint dry white wine

for the sauce
4 tablespoons butter
4 tablespoons flour
1 teacup milk
4 oz freshly peeled cooked
 shrimps
½ lb halved green grapes, with
 pips removed

Ask the fishmonger to clean and fillet the soles. You should have twelve fillets. Make sure you obtain the heads and bones. Season the fillets with ground tarragon, make little rolls of them and fix these with toothpicks.

Make a stock of the heads and bones with the onion, carrot, leek, ½ bay leaf, mace, pepper and salt. Poach the fillets in this stock for 5 minutes at most. Remove the rolls and place them on a dish. Melt the 8 tablespoons butter and gently fry the chopped shallots. Season with salt and pepper, add the wine when the shallots are soft and pale brown; reduce on a low heat until strongly flavoured and almost syrupy.

Melt the remaining 4 tablespoons butter, add the flour in small quantities and make a smooth roux. Cook for 1–2 minutes then add the milk gradually. Bring slowly to simmering point and add the reduced wine. Bring to the boil, stir in the shrimps and remove the pan from the heat immediately. Leave to cool. Stir occasionally to prevent a skin forming.

Cover the fish rolls with grapes, scatter any remaining grapes at the sides and spoon the shrimp sauce over the dish. Leave to cool at room temperature. Do not chill.

dips

Should your buffet still show some bare patches, fill them up with fancy breads, snacks and dips. Remember, too, to keep replacement items for your main dishes in reserve, so that you can keep the platters on your buffet filled, or can replace them.

Here are some 'dips' which you can use either with snacks or as alternative sauces to the ones above.

Dips — an English word which has found great popularity on the Continent! These dips form an excellent start to any party, and are first-class for filling in the spaces on a running buffet or informal supper-table. Whatever the celebration, dips have tremendous advantages, not the least of which is that both the sauces and the dips themselves can be made well in advance.

As a rule, dip 'sauces' are set out in bowls, grouped with breads and other snacks which your guests may want to 'dip'.

Most thick sauces are suitable for dips and vice-versa; in fact practically anything which can be speared on cocktail sticks can be used for dipping.

Among vegetables and fruit, for instance, put out: strips of celeriac, whole spring onions, gherkins, cauliflower sprigs, broccoli spears, button mushrooms, artichoke hearts, melon wedges, chunks of pear and apple, dipped in lemon juice.

As fish: prawns, firmly cooked fish fingers or baby fish cakes, and mussels.

As meat: meat balls, small cooked sausages.

And then: French bread, bread sticks, small bridge rolls, potato crisps, crackers, cheese biscuits and toast fingers.

The simplest dips and sauces are based on mayonnaise, salad cream or a Rémoulade sauce.

With the aid of an electric mixer they can easily be prepared at home, so here are some recipes:

MAYONNAISE

2 egg yolks
½ teaspoon ready-mixed mustard
1½ teaspoon lemon juice
1 teaspoon salt
¼ teaspoon freshly ground pepper
pinch of sugar
½ teaspoon paprika
¾–1 pint olive oil

All the ingredients must be at room temperature, or the mayonnaise may curdle or not thicken at all. Mix the egg yolks with the mustard and the dry ingredients to a smooth paste. Carefully mix in some lemon juice. Then while mixing at speed, trickle in the oil in driblets. Continue until the mayonnaise is as thick as you want it. For a 'dip' sauce, one needs a firm thick mayonnaise.

RÉMOULADE SAUCE

3 hard-boiled eggs
4 tablespoons salad oil
3 tablespoons soured cream
2 tablespoons lemon juice
1 teaspoon ready-mixed mustard
½ teaspoon anchovy paste
1 teaspoon chopped onions
1 chopped gherkin
1 tablespoon capers
1 teaspoon chopped parsley
1 pinch sugar
salt and pepper

Pass the cooled hard-boiled eggs through a sieve. Mix the oil in small quantities into the egg with the electric mixer. Then add the soured cream and lemon juice. Add the remaining ingredients last with the finely chopped egg whites.

This Rémoulade sauce is particularly suitable as a dip sauce for cooked prawns, slices of herring and fish sticks.

RÉMOULADE DIP

1 cup mayonnaise
2 finely chopped hard-boiled eggs
6 chopped stuffed olives
1 tablespoon chopped green pepper
1 clove garlic, squeezed
1 tablespoon anchovy paste
1 teaspoon Worcester sauce
1 teaspoon dry mustard
salt
freshly ground pepper
dry vermouth to taste

Carefully mix the ingredients into the mayonnaise one by one. Finally add to taste the dry vermouth, stir until the sauce is smooth and thick.

CHILLI DIP OR SAUCE

1½ gills mayonnaise
1 tablespoon hot chilli
   sauce
2 tablespoons grated cheese
1 teaspoon powdered,
   crystallized or stem ginger
1 clove squeezed garlic
2 teaspoons finely ground
   dried tarragon
   dash of dry white wine or
   sherry

Carefully mix all the ingredients, blending in one at a time, into the mayonnaise. Serve this dip or sauce with crackers, cheese crackers or French bread. I once served it with miniature pancakes rolled up and cooled, and it tasted unusually good.

CURRY PINEAPPLE DIP OR SAUCE

1 teacup mayonnaise
1 chopped onion
1 clove garlic, squeezed
½ teaspoon curry powder
1 tablespoon cubed pineapple

Mix the mayonnaise carefully with the other ingredients, and scatter some cubed pineapple on the sauce.

Suitable for prawns, cauliflower sprigs or broccoli spears. To make the vegetables more digestible, it may be a good idea to quickly parboil them.

CREAMY TANGERINE DIP OR SAUCE

¾–1 pint condensed cream of
   chicken soup
2 tablespoons single cream
   dash white wine
1 chopped onion
   pinch ground dill
1 6-oz tin tangerines with
   juice
   chopped celery

Mix the unthinned soup with the cream and a dash of white wine. Mix in the chopped onion, the dill and some sections of tangerine without the juice. Mix in the juice last, taking care that the sauce does not become too thin. Dish the remaining tangerine sections on top, and scatter chopped celery over it.

A good sauce for prawns, cold chicken, meat balls, pieces of cooked fish or celery.

MUSHROOM DIP OR SAUCE

1 pint condensed cream of
   mushroom soup
2 tablespoons single cream
1 clove of garlic, squeezed
   paprika
½ teaspoon chopped tarragon
6 button mushrooms
   butter
   salt and pepper

Stir the cream, garlic, paprika and tarragon into the soup. Halve the mushrooms. Fry them lightly in butter, season with pepper and salt. Mix half of them into the sauce and scatter the remainder on top.

This sauce is suitable for strips of fennel root or celeriac, which have been blanched and cooled, and crisps, fried-bread croûtons and cold meat slices.

CHUTNEY MAYONNAISE DIP OR SAUCE

½ pint mayonnaise
¼ pint single cream
2 tablespoons mango chutney
½ chopped onion
   salt and pepper

Mix the mayonnaise with the cream. Chop the mango chutney finely and stir, with the onion, into the mixture. Season with pepper and salt, if necessary.

Serve this sauce with salted, chilled sticks of cucumber or cold small meat balls. It is also excellent with sections of melon or pear.

GARDENERS' DIP OR SAUCE

½ pint mayonnaise
⅛ pint cream
⅛ pint dry sherry
   vegetable juices
1 onion, finely chopped
2 teaspoons mixed cooked
   vegetables
⅛ teaspoon dry mustard
   pinch of ground cumin

Mix all the ingredients carefully; watch that the sauce does not become too thin. Serve this dip or sauce with toast, potato crisps, baby sausages or fish fingers.

LIPTAUER CHEESE DIP OR SAUCE

4 oz cottage or curd cheese
3 tablespoons butter
½ teaspoon anchovy paste
   chopped parsley
1 tablespoon ready-mixed
   mustard
1 chopped onion
   salt and pepper
   paprika
   white wine

Mix all the ingredients except the wine to a smooth paste. Add small quantities of white wine until the consistency you want is obtained.

CUCUMBER DIP OR SAUCE

1 cup mashed, peeled
   cucumber
1 onion, finely chopped
¼ pint soured cream
   pepper
   salt
   finely chopped chives
   pinch of ground cumin

Mix all the ingredients. Beat well with an electric mixer. Leave to cool in the refrigerator. Use as a dip, with cheese crackers, bread sticks fried in garlic butter, rye bread or potato chips; or thin with single fresh cream to make a sauce.

suppers

Most dinner parties at home follow the same more-or-less set pattern. But a supper party can be made a frivolous, happy, uncharted occasion. Of course we can give our friends just fried egg, chips and bacon and then a pudding like they have at home, but this is not the kind of supper I have in mind. My party supper should be light, easily digested, and yet a treat. It need not be large, but what you provide should be delicate and unusual. You should think in terms of dishes which you would not dream of presenting in the ordinary way.

The best supper party of this kind is for two or three at most. It requires candlelight or an old-fashioned lamp, or hidden lighting giving an indirect glow. The table should be laid elegantly in a setting which has real charm — in an alcove, beside the fire or, on a beautiful summer evening, on a terrace or balcony. You serve this kind of supper after a delightful evening at the theatre, or to celebrate a special intimate anniversary.

One drinks a light, frivolous wine with this kind of supper. Champagne or some other sparkling wine is a good choice, or a really good vintage wine.

The following recipes are designed for two people:

menu 1

PÂTÉ MAISON

•

CHICKEN NANTUA

•

BRANDY SNAPS

PÂTÉ MAISON

$3\frac{1}{2}$ oz pâté
$\frac{1}{4}$ pint strong stock
1 tablespoon Madeira or
  port
$\frac{1}{4}$ oz powdered gelatine

Warm the broth, which should be clear and well flavoured. Dissolve the gelatine in the warm broth. Leave to cool, then add the Madeira. Allow to set. Cut the pâté into two thick slices and place on a plate. Cube the set jelly and scatter round the pâté. Serve with hot toast wrapped in a linen napkin.

CHICKEN NANTUA

1 small roasting chicken
  salt
  paprika
$1\frac{3}{4}$ oz butter
  shrimp sauce as served
  with Dover sole on page 74
  single cream
  cognac

Rub the chicken with salt and paprika. Heat most of the butter until a blue haze rises. Seal the chicken in the fat and brown it on all sides. Reduce the heat, add the remaining butter and cook for 45–60 minutes until tender, basting frequently. Make the sauce as described in the recipe and add cream and a few drops of cognac to suit your taste. Divide the chicken into pieces, place them in a small copper pan, pour the sauce on top and place the pan on the table heater on the table. Serve with a crisp green salad.

BRANDY SNAPS

$2\frac{1}{2}$ oz sugar
1 oz butter or margarine
1 oz golden syrup
1 oz plain flour
1 level teaspoon ground
  ginger

Cream sugar, fat and syrup, and stir in the sifted flour and ginger. Make into 12–16 small balls and place really well apart on greased baking sheets. These biscuits spread. Bake in a cool oven (150° C, 310° F, Gas Mark 2) until they are a rich, brown colour. Allow to cool slightly, remove from sheet with a knife and, while still soft enough, roll round the handle of a wooden spoon; remove when set. The snaps should be filled with sweetened and flavoured cream just before serving. Any left over will keep in an airtight tin.

12–16 brandy snaps.

menu 2

CONSOMMÉ ROYALE

•

BLANQUETTE OF VEAL

•

ORANGE FLUMMERY

---

1 pint canned consommé

CONSOMMÉ ROYALE

ROYALE CUSTARD SHAPES

2 egg yolks
salt and pepper
1 tablespoon milk or stock

To make the custard, mix the egg yolks with the seasoning and the milk or stock. Strain it into a small greased basin. Stand the basin in hot water and steam the custard until it is firm. Turn out the custard, cut it into thin slices, and from these cut tiny fancy shapes with a 'brilliant' cutter. Add them to the hot consommé.

BLANQUETTE OF VEAL

1 lb veal, taken from the
shoulder
salt and pepper
1 small onion
bouquet garni
3–4 peppercorns
pinch of grated nutmeg
stock or water
1½ oz butter
1 oz flour
1 egg yolk
2 tablespoons cream or dried
skim milk powder made up
double strength

garnish
croûtes of fried bread or
fleurons of pastry
button mushrooms

Cut the meat into pieces about 2 inches square and put into a stewpan with salt, sliced onion, herbs, peppercorns and nutmeg. Just cover with cold stock or water and simmer until tender — about 2 hours. When the meat is cooked, melt the butter in a saucepan and stir in the flour. Cook for a few minutes without browning. Strain ½ pint liquor from the meat and add to the blended flour and butter. Stir until boiling then simmer for 3 minutes. Beat together the egg yolk and cream or milk and add to the sauce. Stir and cook gently for a few minutes; do not allow to boil or it may curdle. Correct the seasoning. Arrange the meat on a hot dish, piling it high in the centre and strain the sauce over. Garnish with neatly shaped croûtes of fried bread or fleurons of pastry and grilled mushrooms. Serve hot.

ORANGE FLUMMERY

1st layer
3 oz canned orange juice
¾ teaspoon gelatine
½ oz castor sugar

2nd layer
6 oz canned orange juice
1 level teaspoon gelatine
1½ oz castor sugar
1 egg, separated
orange segments
1 level tablespoon cornflour
angelica

Make the first layer by dissolving the gelatine in the orange juice, warmed. Add the sugar and dissolve without boiling. Pour this jelly into the base of a 1-pint mould. Chill to set it.

Make the second layer. Dissolve the gelatine in 4 oz of the juice, warmed. Leave to cool. Blend the cornflour with a little juice, dissolve the sugar by warming it in the rest of the juice, and pour it on the blended cornflour. When the mixture has cooled slightly, beat in the egg yolk. Stir in the dissolved gelatine, trickling it in from a height, whisk the egg white and fold it carefully into the mixture with a wooden spoon. Pour into the mould and leave to set. When the whole is set, turn out carefully, and decorate with orange segments and angelica. An excellent dessert to follow the creamy blanquette.

menu 3

CHICKEN COCKTAIL

•

TONGUE WITH CHERRIES

•

ICED LEMON MERINGUES

CHICKEN COCKTAIL

1 large grapefruit
2 heaped tablespoons finely
chopped cooked chicken
asparagus tips
$\frac{1}{4}$ pint mayonnaise
double cream to taste
sherry to taste
tomato purée to taste
parsley

Halve the grapefruit, remove the flesh and reserve the juice. Chop the flesh finely, and mix with the finely chopped chicken and the asparagus tips. Spoon the mixture into the grapefruit halves. Make a sauce with the mayonnaise, grapefruit juice, double cream, tomato purée and sherry. Pour this on the mixture in the grapefruit halves, and sprinkle some parsley on top. Place the grapefruit halves in compote glasses; place a spoon and fork at the side of each.

TONGUE WITH CHERRIES

1 onion, peeled
1 carrot, scraped
2–3 sprays parsley
1 stick celery
salt to taste
4 peppercorns
1 calf's tongue
white wine to taste
1 oz butter
$\frac{3}{4}$ oz flour
double cream to taste
lemon juice to taste
4 oz canned sour cherries
1 oz toasted, blanched
almonds

Bring a saucepan of water to the boil with the onion, carrot, parsley, celery, salt and peppercorns, and add the tongue. Simmer for 1–1$\frac{1}{2}$ hours until tender. Reserve the stock. Rinse the tongue well under the cold tap, and pull off the skin. Leave to cool, then cut into slices.

Melt the butter, add flour and mix well; then add gradually about $\frac{1}{2}$ pint of the tongue stock, strained. Simmer for 1–2 minutes. Remove from the heat. Mix in the cream, season the sauce with extra salt and pepper, and with the lemon juice. Finally, add the cherries, stoned. Place the slices of tongue on a shallow dish, and pour the warm sauce over them. Reheat over a saucepan of steaming water. Scatter the almonds over the dish just before serving. Steamed rice goes well with the dish.

ICED LEMON MERINGUES

Make or buy two or more individual meringue cases. Just before serving, fill them with lemon sorbet and place a teaspoon of stiffly whipped double cream on top of each. Serve with champagne.

menu 4

PORK VINAIGRETTE WITH MUSHROOMS

•

SALMON CASSEROLE

•

MELON ICECREAM

PORK VINAIGRETTE WITH MUSHROOMS

3½ oz cold, cooked pork, thinly
  sliced
3½ oz mushrooms, chopped
2 tablespoons oil
1 tablespoon vinegar
  pepper to taste
  salt to taste
  dry mustard to taste
  thin brown bread and butter
  parsley
1 shallot, finely chopped

For this first course you need ready-to-serve meat, home-roasted or from a delicatessen, arranged decoratively on a platter. Make a sauce by mixing the oil and vinegar, add salt, freshly ground pepper, dry mustard, some finely chopped shallot and ½ teaspoon chopped parsley. Add the mushrooms, stir once or twice and leave for an hour in a cool place.

Drain the mushrooms well, and serve scattered over the pork. Serve the vinaigrette sauce in a gravy boat, and a dish of thin brown bread and butter.

SALMON CASSEROLE

1 7-oz can red salmon
3–4 oz rice
12 green olives, stoned
1 oz butter
¾ oz flour
1 teaspoon grated onion
1 heaped teaspoon paprika
1 tablespoon grated mild
  cheese
  salt
  barely ½ pint milk

Boil the rice, using your usual recipe. Drain the salmon and carefully remove all bones and skin. Chop it into small pieces.

Cut the olives in halves. Lightly mix the rice, salmon and olives together. Heat the butter; fry the shallot and paprika together until soft, add the flour, fry a minute longer and then gradually add the milk to make a thick sauce. Add salt to suit your taste. Spoon the rice mixture into an ovenproof dish, pour the sauce over it and sprinkle the grated cheese on top. Leave in the oven at 170° C, 325° F, Gas Mark 3 until the cheese has melted. A cucumber salad is ideal with this dish.

MELON ICECREAM

1 small ripe melon
¼ pint vanilla icecream
  crème de menthe liqueur to
  suit your taste

Scoop out the melon flesh with a potato ball cutter. Divide the vanilla icecream into two ice glasses. Spoon the melon balls on top. Pour on a little crème de menthe. Serve with a chilled sparkling white wine.

menu 5

CONSOMMÉ MADRILÈNE

•

FILLETS OF FISH 'EN CUIRASSE'

•

FROMAGE AU CAFÉ

CONSOMMÉ MADRILÈNE

1 pint brown stock
1 lb tomatoes
½ green pepper
½ clove of garlic
  parsley stalks
  thyme
½ bay leaf
¼ lb lean beef
½ carrot
1 egg white
½ onion
½ stick of celery

Cut up the tomatoes and green pepper. Tie the herbs together in a small piece of muslin. Shred and soak the beef in ¼ pint water. Whip the egg white slightly. Put all the ingredients into a pan and simmer very gently for 1 hour. Strain as usual. To garnish cut tiny dice from the firm flesh of skinned tomato. Serve the consommé hot or iced; if iced, it should be almost liquid and may therefore need whisking a little.

FILLETS OF FISH 'EN CUIRASSE'

14 oz deep-frozen fish fillets
  olive oil
  salt
  pepper
1 fennel root
1 redbell pepper
  lemon juice
  brown bread and butter
  green salad

Rub the thawed fillets with olive oil, salt and freshly ground pepper. Cut two pieces of aluminium foil. Brush with olive oil and place some very thin strips of blanched fennel root, and redbell pepper on it. Lay the fish on these. Sprinkle a little lemon juice on the fish and carefully seal the foil, twisting the edges. Place the packets in the oven, preheated to 180° C, 350° F, Gas Mark 4, for 20–30 minutes. Serve the packets still sealed with brown bread and butter slices, and a crisp green salad.

FROMAGE AU CAFÉ

1 teaspoon powdered
  gelatine
1 tablespoon strong cold
  coffee
¾ gill or ⅙ pint hot black
  coffee
  castor sugar to taste
3 oz smooth cream cheese
1 egg white
1 ripe pear, fresh or canned
  double cream

Dissolve the gelatine in the cold coffee, add the hot coffee, sugar, salt and stir until the gelatine is dissolved. Beat the cream cheese with the white of egg until a smooth paste. Gradually stir in the coffee mixture and leave to chill. Serve the cream in tall flute glasses. Peel, halve and core the pear, dip in lemon juice. Place a ripe half pear on top of each glass, and decorate with whipped cream.

This menu requires a dry, aromatic white wine; try Mâcon blanc or an Alsatian Traminer.

menu 6

STUFFED AVOCADO

•

BAKED HAM WITH BANANAS

•

ITALIAN CREAM

STUFFED AVOCADO PEAR

1 avocado pear
a few drops of lemon juice
1 3¾-oz can of crab
1 tomato
½ tablespoon mayonnaise
½ tablespoon soured cream
pinch of cayenne pepper
a few drops of cognac
a few drops of orange juice
sprinkling of tarragon (or parsley), chopped

Cut the avocado pear in half lengthwise and remove the stone. Sprinkle lemon juice on the flesh. Make a sauce by mixing the mayonnaise with the soured cream, a pinch of cayenne, a few drops of cognac and the orange juice. Divide the crab, remove bones and very carefully mix the cut-up tomato with the meat. Spoon the mixture into the avocado pear hollow, and cover with the sauce. If you have fresh tarragon, sprinkle some on top; otherwise use parsley.

BAKED HAM WITH BANANAS

2 thick slices cooked ham
butter
1 large firm banana, peeled and sliced
1 oz brown sugar
2 tablespoons grated coconut
2 tablespoons lemon juice

Cut the fat from the ham, and place the slices in a flameproof dish which has been buttered beforehand. Place a layer of banana slices on top, and sprinkle with lemon juice. Scatter on the brown sugar and the coconut. Dot with butter, and place the dish in a preheated oven at 150° C, 300° F, Gas Mark 2 for half an hour.

With this dish you should serve rice which has been fried quickly in oils and then boiled in stock to which some saffron or a little turmeric and sugar has been added. You can also serve a salad of rings of greenbell pepper sprinkled with oil, vinegar, pepper and salt.

ITALIAN CREAM

½ lemon
¼ pint milk
2 egg yolks or 1 whole egg and 1 yolk
1–2 oz castor sugar
¼ oz gelatine
1½ tablespoons water
¼ pint double cream

Infuse thin strips of the lemon rind in the milk. Beat the eggs and sugar until liquid and make a thick pouring custard with the flavoured milk, straining back into the pan to cook and thicken. Allow to cool. Soak gelatine in the water for 5 minutes, then heat to dissolve. Stir the juice of the lemon gently into the cooled custard, and add the dissolved gelatine, stirring again as it cools. Whip the cream and fold lightly into the custard mixture just before setting.

Pour into a prepared mould and leave to set. If you like, the cream can be poured into individual glass dishes, and decorated according to your own taste.

For vanilla cream, use vanilla essence instead of lemon.

menu 7

HAM WITH SPICED FRUIT

•

VEAL COLLOPS PÉRIGORD

•

PÊCHE MELBA

HAM WITH SPICED FRUIT

This spiced fruit is a speciality from North Italy. It consists of several types of fruit, preserved in a spicy sauce. In this country, you can find them in delicatessen, sold in jars. On two plates lay some thin slices of ham (Ardennes, Wiltshire or York ham) with a spoonful of the fruit.

VEAL COLLOPS PÉRIGOLD

4 veal escalopes, well beaten
salt to suit your taste
2 oz butter
2 oz goose-liver pâté
1 oz butter
¾ oz flour
½ pint veal stock or chicken bouillon
¼ pint white wine
double cream
1 small canned truffle

Fry the escalopes in 2 oz butter on a fairly low heat until just done; they should still be soft and pinkish inside. Keep warm. Make the sauce by melting the 1 oz butter, stir in the flour, then add gradually, still stirring, the stock and wine. Leave to simmer on a very low heat for about 15 minutes. Season if necessary with salt and pepper, and add the cream. Place the veal collops on a dish; place on each 1 oz pâté topped with a slice of truffle. Chop the rest of the truffle and stir it into the sauce; pour over the dish.

This dish is best accompanied by creamed potatoes and sliced green beans. If you put meat on an ovenproof dish, you can pipe the creamed potatoes round the edge in little rosettes, and place the dish in the oven to brown them.

PÊCHE MELBA

2 firm, ripe peaches
½ gill Melba sauce
vanilla essence
2 oz sugar
¼ pint vanilla icecream, home-made or bought

½ pint vanilla icecream
2 canned peach halves
¼ pint Melba sauce
⅛ pint sweetened whipped cream

Halve and peel the peaches. Add the vanilla to the syrup and dissolve the sugar in it. Poach the peaches in the syrup until tender but not broken. Lift out the peaches, drain them on a sieve, and allow to get thoroughly cold. Serve them piled around a mound of vanilla icecream in a silver dish. Set this dish in another dish containing shaved ice. Pour over a rich raspberry syrup, which must be previously iced. Serve at once.

This is the original recipe created in honour of Dame Nellie Melba. It is now often made as follows:

Place a scoop or slice of icecream in 2 sundae glasses. Cover with a peach half. Coat with Melba sauce. Pipe a large rose of cream on top of each.

Other fruits are also used. Pears dipped in lemon juice team well with raspberries, for instance.

barbecues and picnics

In this chapter you will find less about the organization of a barbecue or picnic party than about grilling techniques and what best to take on a picnic. The organization (whether just for the family in the garden, on the deck of a boat, in a field or on the beach or for a large group of friends) is best left to you. It can hardly fail to be a success.

Few things stimulate the appetite better than the scent of a charcoal fire in the open air, of a carefully roasted beefsteak, leg of lamb, chicken leg, lobster tail or even just a hamburger or a sausage.

This was well known to our ancestors. They learned it first when they roasted wild game over a wood fire; just as children learn it by grilling sausages over a tiny fire.

Barbecuing, roasting and grilling, is mainly work for the men, though it does not mean that the womenfolk should be out of reach of the charcoal fire. One would only point out that, when men hear the word barbecue or grill, they suddenly become industrious. The pyromaniac hidden in every man may have something to do with it. Moreover, it seems tough and masculine to eat the products of a charcoal fire. . . .

But what, in fact, *is* roasting? In short, it means to subject the food to direct heat. Thinking of this, we realize straight away that it need not involve prohibitively expensive barbecue equipment. It is enough to have a base and three walls made of small bricks, a grilling grid or sturdy piece of wire netting, charcoal, a long fork or spike, and a brush. To start the fire, you will probably need some methylated spirit; you will also need some good quality oil, a savoury sauce — and then good planning. Good planning means that you must start lighting the charcoal in ample time. The bed of fire is only suitable for roasting when it is reduced to glowing ash. We are inclined to start too quickly on whatever we want to grill, and there is a strong chance of burning the meat or cooking it unevenly. Besides, you will have eaten your steak or chops before the fire is at its best and will remain so for a long time. That seems a pity if good food has not been prepared properly; especially since the quality of the meat must be first-class for barbecuing. That quality is a point you should discuss with your butcher. If he is a good butcher and you tell him how you are going to cook his meat, he will provide the correct cuts.

Besides a simple home-made barbecue grill, many products are made, suitable for outdoor roasting. They range from old-fashioned glazed flameproof pans to expensive barbecues on wheels provided with the latest gadgets such as an adjustable rotisserie unit, roasting skewers, tongs, long forks, etc. Yet, the system remains the same, namely, a flameproof container for the charcoal fire and about 5 inches above that, a metal grid.

When buying a barbecue, bear in mind the number of persons you may want to cook for. You can waste a great deal of charcoal, space and warming-up time by buying a large unit if experience shows that it is used for 4 to 6 people only. On the other hand a small barbecue, such as a Japanese hibachi, is suitable only for half a chicken or satays, or as an additional barbecue.

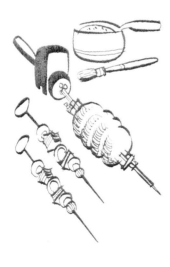

You can of course buy two small barbecues. You are then well equipped for either a large or a small group of people, or for roasting simultaneously various types of food. If you buy an electric rotisserie unit for the barbecue, remember you also need a three-core extension cable to connect it to the nearest socket outlet. So it is best suited to grilling on your verandah, or indoors.

Indoors, too, if you have an open fire with an adequate draught, it may be all right to have a grid on legs or a barbecue placed in it.

Inspect a portable barbecue thoroughly before you buy it. It must be solidly made. Chromed grids have a longer life than thin nickel-plated ones. For preference, you should buy a grid with a small mesh or close-set connection rods. The food is then easier to handle and will

not slip between the bars into the fire. Stoutly built grids will not bend so quickly either.

It is important that the distance between the grid and the fire can be adjusted either by a handle which raises or lowers it automatically or by moving the grid by hand (gloved) to different slots or notches. The result is the same.

As for fuel, charcoal is excellent, as sold by the coal merchant or ironmonger in paper bags. There are also charcoal briquets, which resemble small oval coals; they burn much more evenly than charcoal, but lack the charcoal smell and are far more expensive.

Wood, in well-dried, hard chips, also has a lovely smell, but is much more difficult to light and to keep burning evenly.

Most barbecue containers are deep, so requiring a large amount of charcoal to reach the right level below the grid. So one often shovels a layer of loose sand or gravel into the container before the charcoal or other fuel, spreading it as evenly as possible. The sand and the gravel protect the base of the container against over-heating and also reflect the heat upwards as well as reducing fuel waste. But of course this can only be done at home.

Use as little methylated spirit or petrol as possible to start your fire. If necessary, fan it or give it a draught with a bicycle pump, to get it going. Out of doors, a slight breeze may be of benefit. If the barbecue has a semi-circular windscreen, place it with the open side towards the direction from which the wind comes until the charcoal is well alight. Then turn the screen towards the wind.

If you have a loose grid on your barbecue, only place it on the fire when it is well alight. If you have a fixed one, place it at its highest position for the lighting. This enables you to spread the burning charcoal a little, if necessary.

When using charcoal as the fuel, the brighter the glow, the greater the heat, especially when the pieces of charcoal are packed tightly together or in a high pile. In order to reduce the heat, spread the charcoal out a little or place the grid at a greater distance from the fire.

Ovenproof gloves will prove very useful when managing a barbecue.

When you put the food in place for grilling, do not overload the grid. It makes turning the meat over difficult. Brush lean meat or fish with oil or barbecue sauce, and watch the food carefully. Drips of oil may fall into the fire and make flames spurt up which burn the food. If this happens, damp them with water — or beer.

Talking about sauces: do not be too liberal. The meat should be good enough on its own. Do not make many sauces either. One to brush over the food during the grilling is enough, and one or two more to serve with the grilled food.

Only use for a barbecue shellfish, fish, meat, birds and game of the best quality. If you only brush the food with oil, use the best salad oil or olive oil. Season the food after grilling more than usual; grilled food can stand it. Never salt the meat before you place it on the barbecue; the salt draws the meat juices, and makes the meat damp on the surface. Result: tough meat. Dry the outside of meat with a clean cloth or a firm paper napkin. Brush it with your oil, butter or barbecue sauce, and grill it unseasoned. Add the seasoning later. If you use a barbecue sauce which has been salted, it may not need any. A good steak is excellent when only roasted brushed with melted butter and seasoned with some pepper, chopped parsley and some garlic, and perhaps a dash of cognac or red wine.

Be very careful not to spoil the meat by over-grilling. This is most likely to occur with veal or pork, which must be well done. One tends to leave them too long. Rather make the heat of the charcoal fire a little less fierce than usual, so that the meat can stay on the grid a little longer. When using a barbecue, experience is the best teacher.

For this reason, let us now turn to some recipes for sauces to brush on the food.

PARSLEY BUTTER SAUCE

$\frac{1}{4}$ lb butter
2 tablespoons chopped
  parsley
1 tablespoon lemon juice
$\frac{1}{2}$ teaspoon freshly ground
  black pepper
$\frac{1}{4}$ teaspoon thyme, ground

Melt the butter in a small pan with a heavy base. Chop the parsley very fine and mix with the melted butter, add lemon juice, ground pepper and the thyme. The sauce is then ready for brushing on.

If you replace the parsley by celery, you have a completely different sauce, excellent for fish, and if you replace it by ground cumin, the sauce is perfect for use on a juicy pork cutlet. The lemon juice can be replaced by orange, tangerine or pineapple juice. A dash of Worcester sauce can be added for yet another variation.

Incidentally, the best way to grill fish is on a piece of aluminium foil.

SPICED SOY SAUCE

$\frac{1}{4}$ pint soy sauce (bottled)
$\frac{1}{4}$ pint sherry or whisky
$\frac{1}{4}$ pint salad oil
1 clove of garlic, squeezed
$\frac{1}{4}$ teaspoon ground ginger

Mix all the ingredients; this sauce is excellent either for brushing on or for marinating meat or game. If the meat is not quite as juicy as it should be, it can be marinated for half a day or longer. Dry it thoroughly before grilling. The sauce can also be used for shellfish. Salad oil can be replaced by corn oil if necessary. A sprinkling of ground aniseed gives a surprisingly pleasant flavour.

HONEY–SOY SAUCE

$\frac{1}{8}$ pint honey
$\frac{1}{4}$ pint stock
$\frac{1}{8}$ pint soy sauce
2 tablespoons tomato
  ketchup
$\frac{1}{4}$ teaspoon ground ginger
$\frac{1}{2}$ clove of garlic, squeezed

Mix all ingredients and simmer for about 10 minutes on a low heat. Excellent for a leg of lamb, chicken or turkey. If the quantity of sauce is increased slightly, it can afterwards be completed with some good tomato sauce, or chilli sauce and finely chopped onion. You can then serve this sauce with the grilled food, whether the kinds above or rib of pork, frankfurters, sausages or slices of ham.

PEPPER SAUCE

$\frac{1}{8}$ pint olive oil
1 clove garlic, squeezed
3 redbell peppers
$\frac{1}{2}$ teaspoon salt
2 tablespoons white wine
  vinegar or lemon juice
$\frac{1}{4}$ teaspoon ground cumin

Heat the olive oil in a small pan and fry the garlic in it. Add the finely chopped peppers from which the seeds have been removed, and cook gently. Add the remaining ingredients and stir well. A suitable sauce for fish, meat and birds.

SPICY BARBECUE SAUCE

$\frac{1}{8}$ pint olive oil
generous $\frac{1}{4}$ pint chopped
onion
1 clove of garlic, squeezed
$\frac{1}{2}$ pint honey
$\frac{1}{2}$ pint tomato ketchup
$\frac{1}{4}$ pint red wine vinegar, or
more to taste
$\frac{1}{8}$ pint Worcester sauce, or
more to taste
1 tablespoon dry English
mustard
$1\frac{1}{2}$ teaspoons salt
1 teaspoon ground oregano
or marjoram
1 teaspoon black pepper
$\frac{1}{2}$ teaspoon ground thyme

Heat the oil in a small pan. Add the onion and garlic and fry until the onion is soft. Add all other ingredients, bring to boil while stirring. Simmer for another 5 minutes on a very low heat. This sauce can be kept in sealed jars. Suitable for hamburgers, frankfurters, steaks and rib of pork.

TOMATO SAUCE

1 large onion
1 clove of garlic
$\frac{1}{4}$ pint olive oil
$3\frac{1}{2}$ oz mushrooms
$\frac{1}{4}$ teaspoon salt
$\frac{1}{2}$ teaspoon oregano or
marjoram
$\frac{1}{2}$ teaspoon ground tarragon
$1\frac{1}{4}$ lb peeled tomatoes
1 oz chopped stuffed olives
$\frac{1}{4}$ pint chutney
2 tablespoons chopped
parsley

Chop the onion and garlic, and fry for 5 minutes in the oil, until soft. Boil the finely chopped mushrooms in a little water and salt as quickly as possible. Add them to the onion with all the remaining ingredients except the parsley. Leave to simmer for about 15 minutes, and sprinkle the chopped parsley over. Serve this sauce with grilled spare ribs, hamburgers, steaks or meat balls.

VERMOUTH SAUCE

$\frac{1}{4}$ pint olive oil
$\frac{1}{4}$ pint red vermouth
2 teaspoons salt
$\frac{1}{8}$ teaspoon pepper

Stir all ingredients well together and use the sauce without cooking it, to brush the meat or fish.

A barbecue party is not complete without satays. These satays used to be served with Indonesian rice dishes, but now they have become a favourite delicacy at barbecue parties as well. They are served like smaller versions of the well-known kebabs. So here are recipes for both.

PRAWN KEBABS

24 deep-frozen unshelled
prawns
1 large onion
1 small onion
1 clove of garlic, squeezed
1 teaspoon chilli powder
$\frac{1}{4}$ teaspoon ground fennel
1 tablespoon lemon juice
2 tablespoons sherry
2 tablespoons oil

Thaw the prawns in a colander, peel them and dry them with a clean cloth or paper serviette. Remove the black gut from the back. Grate the onion and mix with the other ingredients. Brush the prawns with this mixture and leave them for a while. Thread them on skewers, and grill them, turning once.

SPICY SATAYS

just over 1 lb juicy fat
meat (pork fillet, loin of
lamb)
6 kemirie nuts (Indian
walnuts) or walnuts,
finely ground
10 small onions
2 cloves of garlic
1 tablespoon anchovy paste
1 teaspoon tamarind
chutney
1 tablespoon soft brown
sugar
$\frac{1}{2}$ teaspoon ground
coriander
$\frac{1}{4}$ teaspoon ground cumin
salt
pepper
salad oil

Cut the meat into 1-inch cubes. Toss all the other ingredients together except the salt, pepper and oil.

Mix the meat well with the spicy mixture and thread the cubes on the skewers. Leave them for a while. Season them with salt and pepper. Brush some oil on the satays and grill, turning the skewers frequently.

SATAYS OF CRAB

1 7-oz can of crab
3 slices of white bread
without crusts
milk, and crab juice from
can to moisten
1 egg yolk
pepper to taste
grated nutmeg to taste
ground cumin to taste
1 clove of garlic, squeezed
chopped parsley to taste
chopped leek to taste

Remove the crab from the can and keep the liquid. Mash the crab finely with a fork and remove the bones. Soak the slices of bread in a little milk and the crab juice until soft. Mix all ingredients well and roll into small balls, about 1-inch in diameter. Thread them on skewers. Brush melted butter on the balls and grill them carefully on the barbecue.

In the gay nineties picnics were the order of the day. Many painters immortalized the gay get-togethers on their canvases.

Such a party requires little effort. The advance preparation is the major part of the work. You can pack all your ingredients into plastic bags or foil, put everything in a heavy basket, and cover it with a gay cloth which can later serve as a tablecloth, or rather ground-cloth. Provide coffee in a vacuum flask, beakers, bread, smoked fish, cold meat, cheese, butter, a bottle of wine, a sharp knife and some paper napkins and you are already a long way towards a festive meal.

There are also beautiful picnic baskets on the market, equipped with cutlery, plates, beakers, board, etc. There are, too, refrigerated bags which keep the food and drinks, salad and fruit cold for the greater part of the day. One can even take a calor-gas cooker, to finish the cooking of a pre-roasted chicken in the open air, or a barbecue to do one's own grilling outside.

The preparation can, of course, be divided amongst several participants. So let us see that else we can put in the basket:

CHICKEN WITH OLIVES

2 baby chickens
salt
pepper
butter and olive oil
2 large onions
1 clove of garlic, squeezed
ground thyme to taste
2–3 tablespoons tomato
ketchup
1 3-oz glass sherry or
vermouth
a few black olives, stoned

Rub the chickens, inside and out, with salt, pepper and half melted butter, half oil. Roast gently until golden brown and tender. Cut them in half, lengthwise. Chop the onions and fry them with the garlic, thyme and ketchup in the butter used for roasting the chicken, until the onions are soft. Add the sherry and olives and simmer for a few moments with the halved chickens. Leave to cool. When quite cold, place everything in a foil container. The chickens can be reheated on the picnic spot if you take a heater with you.

ROAST PIGEONS

4 pigeons
16 ½-inch cubes of cooked
bacon joint or salt belly
of pork
1 onion
butter
salt
pepper
ground thyme to taste
shredded rosemary to
taste
white wine

Stuff each of the pigeons with 4 cubes of bacon or pork, a quarter onion, a ½-inch cube of butter and some of the herbs. Rub the outside with more of the herbs and butter and fry them on a moderate heat until brown on all sides. Mix the frying butter with a little white wine and leave the birds to cook in this. When cold, place the birds and sauce in a foil container. On arrival at the picnic spot, transfer them again to a pan with a lid, or simply reheat the foil dish if suitable. Add a little more wine and a cube of butter with some extra herbs to suit your taste, and leave to cook until tender.

You can continue filling the basket for this outdoor party with a 'starter' course comprising some smoked trout with garlic mayonnaise; also take different kinds of bread, sausage, lettuce, tomatoes and some fruit for 'afters'. However, if you want to have a hot first course (say before a football match, on a blustery day) what about . . .

FRIED SCAMPI WITH OREGANO BUTTER

12 deep-frozen scampi
4½ oz butter
2 teaspoons dried oregano
pepper and salt
olive oil
miniature bottle dry
white vermouth

Thaw the scampi in a colander. Peel and clean them, and remove the black spine if uncooked. Split down the front and stuff with some butter mixed with the oregano, pepper and salt. Pack the stuffed scampi in aluminium foil and store in a refrigerator or bag. At the picnic place, rub a little olive oil over the frying pan and sauté the scampi in this over moderate heat for a few moments, until they 'blush' and turn a golden-brown colour. Add the vermouth, and eat at once, straight from the pan, with some French bread and a little garlic mayonnaise.

If you cannot take a heater with you, remember that really hot soup in a vacuum flask makes a good first course.

As a final extra item of luggage for a picnic, do not forget a large plastic jug with clean water to rinse the cutlery quickly and a spare empty large plastic bag in which to take home your empty boxes and paper, etc.

breakfast parties

In this country, we are not yet accustomed to the idea of inviting guests for a festive breakfast. But it is becoming quite a usual event in the United States and it is beginning to 'catch on' in Europe and here. At the moment, it is being tried out mainly by businessmen. Following the famous 'press breakfasts' at the White House, the attempts are being made to organize press conferences between nine and ten in the morning and to serve breakfast with them.

Besides this 'working' breakfast gathering, there are a number of cheaper business breakfasts for early office workers and for those who cannot be bothered to make breakfast for themselves at home.

However, a true breakfast party, when one invites friends and acquaintances to a festive breakfast on Sunday morning is different, and is a late meal or 'brunch' party which replaces breakfast and lunch. It has much in its favour, especially in summer, if one lives in the country or if one has a swimming pool. It is a good idea too, if one is usually busy in the evenings.

A Sunday breakfast or brunch party starts at about eleven o'clock, and as far as food and drinks are concerned, it is a cross between a generous breakfast and a snack or buffet lunch. Indoors, the dishes are usually all set out on the sideboard (hot ones on plate-warmers or heater trays); the guests help themselves and find their own places at the table with their plate, cup or glass. The idea is that they return to the sideboard several times for another choice. Out of doors, a buffet table can be used, or helpers can hand round food on trays.

This kind of breakfast party is completely informal. You do not wait for late arrivals, for instance; they may have overslept, and never come.

Here are some savoury, warm dishes which are well suited to a breakfast or 'brunch' party, especially during winter. These are prepared in the kitchen and kept warm.

CHICKEN LIVERS WITH MUSHROOMS

2 tablespoons butter
1 onion
2½ teaspoons paprika
  salt
  pepper
  flour
1 lb chicken livers
½ lb mushrooms, halved
  parsley
  dash of sherry

Melt the butter and sauté the chopped onion and paprika. Add the chicken livers which have been dredged with a little flour, salt and pepper. Stir well, add the halved mushrooms and the sherry. Leave to simmer for about 8 minutes. Sprinkle some parsley on the top.

KEDGEREE

1 lb cold cooked fish
  (smoked haddock is
  generally preferred)
$\frac{1}{4}$ lb rice
2 hard-boiled eggs
2 oz butter
  salt and pepper
  cayenne pepper

Boil and dry the rice. Divide the fish into small flakes. Cut the whites of the eggs into slices and sieve the yolks. Melt the butter in a saucepan, add to it the fish, rice, egg whites, salt, pepper and cayenne and stir until hot. Turn the mixture on to a hot dish. Press into the shape of a pyramid with a fork, decorate with egg yolk and serve as hot as possible.

There are two types of omelet: the French, which is flat and generally served folded into three, and the English which is fluffy and more like a soufflé.

The essentials in making either type are a thick, clean and dry omelet pan of the right size, i.e. 6–7 inches diameter for a 2- or 3-egg omelet; butter; eggs; and seasoning.

For savoury omelets, use one of the two basic types, and fill or stuff the omelet before folding with a small amount of grated cheese, cooked meat or fish, with a little creamy sauce if liked.

FRENCH OMELETTE

2–3 eggs
  salt and pepper
$\frac{1}{2}$ oz butter

Break the eggs into a basin. Add salt and pepper to taste. Beat the eggs with a fork until they are lightly mixed. Heat the butter in the pan and slowly let it get hot, but not so hot that the butter browns. Without drawing the pan off the heat, pour in the egg mixture. It will cover the pan and start cooking at once.

Shake the pan and stir the eggs with a fork away from the side to the middle. Shake again. In about 1 minute the omelette will be soft but no longer runny. Let it stand for 4 or 5 seconds for the bottom to brown slightly. Then remove from the heat. Using a palette knife, fold the omelette from two sides over the middle. Then slip on to a hot dish, or turn it upside down on to the dish.

This omelette can be eaten plain, or it can be filled. There are two methods of filling; flavouring such as herbs or cheese can be added to the eggs after they are beaten, or they can be added to the omelette just before it is folded.

ENGLISH OMELETTE OR OMELET

Separate the eggs. Add half an egg-shell of water for each egg, to the yolks: beat them with a wooden spoon until creamy. Whisk the whites until they stay in the basin when turned upside down. Gently fold the whites into the yolks. Have the butter ready in the pan as for the French omelette. Pour in the egg mixture, and cook until it is golden-brown on the underside. Then put the pan under the grill and lightly brown the top. Fillings are usually spread over the cooked omelet. Now run a palette knife round the edge of the pan. Fold the omelet over and slip on to a hot dish.

One or two variations on the well-known scrambled eggs theme must not be overlooked. To the beaten egg mixture and cream (for 12 eggs, use $\frac{1}{4}$ pint double cream) add:

finely chopped fresh green herbs, such as chives, chervil, parsley, shallot;

finely chopped ham or salami;

grated cheese;

cubed fried bread and crumbled or diced fried bacon;

garden peas and finely chopped redbell peppers or tomato.

Alternatively, make an oven dish, such as:

EGGS AU GRATIN

6 hard-boiled eggs
1 oz flour
1$\frac{1}{4}$ oz butter
$\frac{1}{8}$ pint milk and cream, mixed
1 lb cooked ham
1 onion, chopped
1 teaspoon curry powder or paste
grated cheese to taste
golden breadcrumbs as topping
butter

Make a thick sauce by stirring the flour into the melted butter and adding the milk and cream. Brown a very finely chopped onion with the curry powder or paste in a little more butter. Add this to the sauce. Place the halved eggs with the flat side downwards in a buttered flameproof dish. Scatter the finely chopped or diced ham between. Pour on the white sauce and finally the golden breadcrumbs and grated cheese. Dot with butter and leave to brown in the oven.

In winter, savoury apples may be popular. . . .

BAKED APPLES, SAVOURY

Peel and core the apples. Split the skins horizontally round the middle. Fill the centres with a mixture of grated mild cheese and raisins, or with sausage meat; for a fish dish, use flaked smoked haddock, lemon juice, and butter. Place the apples in a flameproof dish, pour some melted butter over them and bake in a moderate oven, at 180° C, 350° F, Gas Mark 4, until tender. Serve on a hot dish.

Another winter favourite is:

SAVOURY BATTER

4 oz flour
1 egg
½ pint milk
4 tablespoons finely chopped
   beef or mutton
   salt and pepper
1 teaspoon finely chopped
   parsley
½ teaspoon mixed herbs

Mix the flour, egg, milk, salt and pepper into a smooth batter, let it stand for ½ hour. Then add the meat, parsley and herbs. Melt a little dripping in a Yorkshire pudding tin. Pour in the batter, and bake in a fairly hot oven (190° C, 375° F, Gas Mark 5) until set.

The final touches to your 'brunch' sideboard are to add a tray of cheeses, smoked meats, bacon or ham, hot cocktail sausages, and for those with a sweet tooth, rolls, honey and marmalade. Add bowls of butter balls, and finally various breads: croissants, French bread, rye bread, brown bread and thin slices of white bread or toast.

In June, a glorious large bowl of strawberries and a jug of cream make a wonderful addition.

The most festive form of breakfast party is a champagne breakfast; the guests are received with a glass of champagne (many people say that champagne tastes best in the morning at 11 o'clock) and drink it with various light dishes or cakes. This was a commonplace custom 100 years ago; but now we give this kind of party to celebrate something especially joyful. For those with a 'tight' budget, a good vin mousseux can equally well be served or in winter a red wine at room temperature. Whatever you choose, the bottles are placed on the sideboard or bar; white wines should be in attractive coolers; but if you do not have these, or not enough of them, you can use plastic buckets filled with water and ice cubes, around which you drape a clean white napkin.

For a less extravagant breakfast party, the following drinks could be served. To welcome the guests, you can serve a glass of sherry. Sherry is a good morning drink, as long as it is dry and of a light variety, such as Manzanilla. Follow it with fruit juices, for example orange juice and tomato juice in glass jugs with ice cubes, and then hot coffee and tea.

A very acceptable drink to start this kind of party is also:

SHERRY FLIP

Shake together in a cocktail shaker,
¼ pint sherry, 1 egg, 1 tablespoon crushed ice, 1 teaspoon sugar and possibly a dash of cognac. Serve this delicious foaming drink in a wide glass with a grating of nutmeg dusted on top.

a party in your new house

What better reason for a party than to 'christen' a new house? You have probably been waiting for months to get ownership or for the builders to finish; but at long last the time for a house-warming has arrived; a party to be shared by your family and nearest and dearest friends, because by its nature it is a very intimate party.

The main problem in giving a house-warming party is usually two conflicting wishes: your wish to give a party, and your desire to protect a new floor covering, furniture, etc. One quite novel but practical solution is to give a party on the bare floor, before the furniture has been moved in, or even before any necessary alterations have been carried out.

This solution also presents some problems; but they are not really very difficult to solve. The tables you need can be trestle tables covered with paper tablecloths. Guests who want to sit down can do so on the removal crates.

As long as there is water and electricity or gas for heating, all is well. The dishes can be made in the old house; for instance, make a large tureen of soup, which can be kept warm in vacuum flasks in the new house. Other easy-to-make snacks can be kept in refrigerator bags with hot (boiled) bags of dry ice. For serving, an easy solution is to use paper plates and dishes, which can be thrown away afterwards — and eliminate your washing-up problem.

It is, of course, essential to keep everything as simple as possible. The atmosphere is already 'something special'. Limit yourself mostly to cold snacks: herring and French cheese for instance. The food can also include a home-made pâté, which can be prepared beforehand. Do not forget to have French bread, butter, hard-boiled eggs, bowls of mayonnaise, salt, pepper, tomato or mushroom ketchup, a whole liver sausage, etc. as well as meat balls, croquettes, sausage rolls. Get flagons of beer and let the guests help themselves; or buy a pipkin or casquette of cheap red wine from which everyone can fill their glass.

In a large house, you need not limit the numbers stringently; but in a small house or a flat, it is essential to keep the numbers down or you will find yourself giving an unofficial standing reception. Otherwise, spread them out by asking some early and some late; invite them just to call in to wish the new house well.

If you describe the type of party beforehand, your guests will not stay longer than half an hour or an hour, and you will be able to cope with most of your friends.

However, do not forget the intimacy of this type of party, which means that only your real friends should be invited.

at the end of the party

The party has been a success! Numerous bottles have been uncorked, numerous dishes consumed. There is a pleasant atmosphere of people who have shared drinks and enjoyed good food.

The record player plays a last disc and somebody makes a point about farewells — many a wise word is spoken under those circumstances, when the candles are nearly burnt out.

The time of departure draws near but no one is quite prepared to leave. Everyone lingers. So this is the moment for the hostess to vanish into the kitchen, and reappear with a large tray of steaming hot soup bowls. It is an elegant way to say that the moment to leave really has arrived.

This good-night soup for the early hours is best made beforehand, so that it only needs reheating. There are now extremely attractive soup tureens and jugs available, in which the soup can both be heated and gratinated in the oven. Place individual bowls in the bottom of the oven to warm. Then put each on a paper napkin on a plate and warn your guests that both soup and bowl are really hot.

Actually, the idea of finishing a delightful evening with a cup of hot soup originates from the Paris markets. In the early hours one used frequently to see parties in evening dress enjoying a cup of real French onion soup with the market hands in the small bistros near the market. This is why we start these few suggestions for a heartwarming farewell with . . .

FRENCH ONION SOUP (8 cups)

8 onions
2 tablespoons butter
1 tablespoon flour
2 teaspoons sugar
  salt
  pepper
4 pints stock
8 slices French bread
  grated cheese

Cut the onions into thin rings. Melt the butter and fry the onions dusted with the flour and sugar until golden-yellow, stirring occasionally. Add the salt and freshly ground pepper. Leave to simmer for some 20 minutes. Toast the slices of French bread and place them at the bottom of an ovenproof tureen (or one each in 8 oven-proof individual soup bowls). Pour the hot soup on the bread, making it float. A thick layer of grated cheese finishes the soup (use Gruyère cheese for preference) and brown the cheese in a hot oven.

As a variation, add some white wine before the stock; or fry a few cloves of garlic with the onion, and make the soup more spicy by the addition of a pinch of cayenne pepper. Before putting the soup in the oven, you can likewise add some whisked egg yolks, or for something very special, add some finely chopped nuts just before serving.

Onion soup is extremely useful for a pleasant return to practical life after a merry evening's drinking.

HUNGARIAN SAUERKRAUT SOUP (8 cups)

1 lb canned sauerkraut
$1\frac{3}{4}$ oz diced lean bacon
2 large onions
2 teaspoons paprika
3 oz butter
2 oz flour
4 pints vegetable stock
1 Hungarian sausage
1 carton soured cream

Just as in Paris many a party ends with onion soup, so in Hungary the farewells are said with a bowl of sauerkraut soup. Sauerkraut soup has the same freshening and sobering effect as the onion soup.

Steam the sauerkraut over simmering water. Fry the diced bacon and the finely chopped onions and paprika in 1 oz of the butter, and add to the sauerkraut. Melt the remaining butter and fry the flour gently until golden-yellow. Add a little of the stock, blend the mixture to a paste and then add to the rest of the stock. Cut the sausage in slices and leave in the soup to simmer for a few minutes. Mix sauerkraut into the stock. Serve continental rye bread with this soup.

OXTAIL SOUP FROM THE AUVERGNE (8 cups)

1 oxtail
  piece of bacon rind or
  pork skin from joint,
  6–8 inches square
1 carrot, chopped
1 onion, chopped
1 stick celery, sliced
16–20 dried chestnuts,
  soaked
1 bundle parsley stalks
4 pints water
$3\frac{1}{2}$ oz diced bacon, cooked
2 tablespoons cooked
  haricot beans
  butter
$\frac{1}{4}$ pint white wine
1 bay leaf
  pinch of thyme
  parsley to sprinkle

Cut the oxtail into joints and lay in a baking tin covered with the rind. Pack the vegetables round them. Leave in a low oven to sweat for $\frac{1}{4}$ hour. Transfer all the ingredients to a large saucepan, add the herbs and water and simmer for about 3 hours. After $1\frac{1}{2}$ hours add the chestnuts. Strain. Remove the meat from the oxtail bones, cube and return to the soup. Add the white wine, beans and diced bacon and the chestnuts. Leave to simmer for another $\frac{1}{4}$ hour. Sprinkle liberally with parsley.

CRAB SOUP WITH CROÛTES (8 cups)

1½ oz butter
1¼ oz flour
4 pints fish stock, chicken or vegetable
2 7¾-oz cans of crab meat
1 tablespoon butter
1 onion, chopped
2 teaspoons paprika
1 tablespoon tomato purée
2–3 tablespoons cooked rice
pinch cayenne pepper
2 tablespoons cognac
2–3 tablespoons dry white breadcrumbs
2–3 tablespoons grated Cheddar cheese

Melt the 1½ oz butter, mix in the flour and leave to turn golden-yellow over very low heat. Stir in the stock and leave to simmer. Remove the bones from the crab and divide into small pieces. Melt the tablespoon of butter, fry the finely chopped onion with the paprika and the crab. Add this to the stock. Mix in the tomato purée, the cayenne pepper and the rice. Leave to simmer for a minute or two, add the cognac. Divide the soup between the soup bowls, or transfer the soup to large ovenware tureens. Scatter a mixture of very dry breadcrumbs and grated cheese over and leave in a very hot oven for a few minutes to brown on top. If the soup is prepared beforehand, add the cognac just before the reheating, but do not let the soup boil.

Instead of the breadcrumbs and cheese, you then spoon one tablespoon of soured cream into each individual bowl and sprinkle some parsley and paprika on top.

ITALIAN FISH SOUP (8 cups)

4–6 tablespoons olive oil
1 lb deep-frozen fish fillets, thawed and skinned
4 carrots, cleaned and chopped
1 large leek, cleaned and sliced
2 cloves of garlic, mashed
4 potatoes, cleaned, peeled and diced
2 onions, peeled and chopped
1 tablespoon olive oil
1 tablespoon tomato purée
¼ pint white wine
pepper
salt
sprinkling of parsley
8 slices bread without crusts
butter
8 slices pecovino cheese
pinch of paprika

Heat the olive oil and quickly fry the finely chopped vegetables until soft. Cut the fish fillets into strips. Place the fillet strips on top of the vegetables, pour on the white wine mixed with the tomato purée and leave to simmer for some minutes, then add about 4 pints water. Leave to simmer for about 20 minutes. Season with salt and pepper and sprinkle liberally with parsley. Spread the slices of bread with butter, place the slices of cheese on top, dust this well with paprika and put the slices in a hot oven or under a grill flame for a few moments until the cheese is melted. Cut the slices into strips and hand round on a plate with the soup.

children's parties

If you want to give a child a happy memory for life, organize a fantastic children's party.

No memory is more cherished than the one of that very special party, when all one's friends — and oneself — were treated to exciting surprises.

This, however, can be a real problem for parents: in our hurried modern lives, we do not give ourselves time to think of something very special and then to work out how to organize it. Yet, if the planning goes wrong, the best ideas can fall flat.

Another problem is that many homes are too small to organize a really good children's party on any scale. Children need room to run about. This is why the out-of-doors party is becoming more and more popular:

a visit to the zoo, a fun fair, a pantomime or cinema. Yet this type of outing may be an improverishment, if the child himself no longer participates in the planning and organizing. Some parents like to keep a birthday child, for instance, away from the preparations in order to make the surprises complete; on the other hand, the child may be stimulated by participating. The choice depends on the age of the child, his inclinations, and the imagination and patience of the parents.

If he wants to share your plans, prepare the day's treats the day before, in consultation with the child, so that at least on that score there are no unnecessary worries. Room decoration such as paper chains make a cheerful background, the more colourful the better. Even if you use the same chains year in, year out, the child will always get a very special feeling when the decorations appear. This ritual is important, especially if the actual birthday party is not given on the day itself, owing to school hours.

We will concentrate mainly on birthday parties, because his birthday is the most important day in the life of a child.

In many continental households he is festively awakened and then led in triumph to a decorated chair in order to receive the good wishes and presents of the family. However, the 'awakening' part is usually a convention only, as the child is usually awake at break of day from pure excitement about the coming events.

When, after a breakfast, chosen by himself, the child goes to school, he can carry a treat for the teacher and his or her classmates. Such a treat depends greatly on the fashion of the moment. Some kinds of sweets are suddenly 'in' and equally suddenly other ones are no longer popular. But a plain cake or sugared biscuits are a good alternative. You can put the goodies in an ordinary bag; but why not a gaily painted basket, which — you must admit — looks much better.

a breakfast for the birthday child

FRESH APPLE

•

MILK SHAKE

•

A GAY OPEN SANDWICH, INCLUDING
SCRAMBLED EGG

•

A SLICE OF CAKE

Pre-school children are usually at their best and most active in the morning; so why not organize a morning party? It is bound to be a success. Don't make it last too long. Turn it into a 'coffee morning' for the mothers, and for the toddlers make it a . . .

Leave the birthday child to make his own choice of milk shake: it is part of the festivities of the day. The open sandwich, too. Use one of the delightful Danish ones pictured in many books. This is a festive way to present the child with healthful breakfast foods, to start the busy day ahead. The slice of cake is an 'extra', for a treat.

zoo party

Lay the table with a gay paper tablecloth, and put out cardboard plates and beakers. Decorate the table with party hats, because it belongs to the tradition. However, don't be surprised if some little ones refuse to put the hats on. Make, instead of the traditional birthday cake with candles, some pastries in the shapes of dogs, cats, chickens, mice, etc., or buy 'animal biscuits'. Make the table centrepiece a large stuffed toy animal, with little gifts for the guests pinned to it, which are given out at the end of the 'meal'.

If you are going to organize games, remove the toys of the birthday child from the scene. Children are very distracted by toys, and will not concentrate on the games. Moreover, there is always the chance of a 'free for all' when they suddenly all decide to want the same toy.

However, most very small children prefer free play to set games, so do not be too rigid about planning their activities.

Have a free flow of fresh orange juice and milk, kept ready in jugs, throughout the party. For older children, games are more popular; even so, they must not last too long. Alternate busy games with quiet ones. The children like a change. Make a programme of the games you wish to play. Set everything out ready for the game and secure the assistance of another adult, even if the number of little guests is not very great.

It is a good idea for the parents to have a mutual agreement not to give presents costing more than a certain amount; otherwise the present-giving turns into a pressing obligation or even competition, and the child gets spoiled in the process. The originality of the present is much more important than the cost. What about a birthday party lunch instead of the usual 'tea'? Give it on a Saturday or Sunday, and serve a menu the children will know, such as:

CHICKEN JOINTS, BAKED OR GRILLED

•

APPLE SAUCE

•

POTATO CHIPS

•

ICECREAM OR A GÂTEAU

With this menu, serve Coca cola, if the parents allow it, and also plenty of fruit juice.

If a child's birthday is in the summer, you can take the young guests outside and have a festive picnic snack party. Among all the snacks you think of, do not forget to take a lot of fresh fruit. It is good for them. Remember, too, that the fresh air makes children thirsty.

When celebrating outside, provide adequate adult supervision and again draw up a programme, which you should follow as much as possible.

As most children like icecream, here are some simple recipes for home-made icecream:

2 lb loaf sugar
1 pint water

SYRUP FOR WATER ICES

Place the sugar and water in a strong saucepan. Allow the sugar to dissolve over gentle heat. Do not stir. When the sugar has dissolved, gently boil the mixture for 10 minutes, or, if a saccharometer is available, until it registers about 100° C, 200° F. Remove scum as it rises. Strain, cool and store. 1 pint syrup.

LEMON WATER ICE

6 lemons
2 oranges
1½ pints syrup, as above

Peel the fruit thinly and place the rind in a basin. Add the hot syrup, cover and cool. Add the juice of the lemons and oranges. Strain, chill and freeze.

LEMON OR ORANGE SORBET

1 pint water
8 oz loaf sugar
2 egg whites
½ pint lemon or orange juice

Dissolve the sugar in the water. Boil for 10 minutes, strain and cool. Add the juice and stiffly whisked egg whites. Freeze and serve at once.

BASIC ICECREAM CUSTARDS

1 economical
1 oz custard powder
1 pint milk
4 oz castor sugar

Blend the custard powder with a little of the milk. Boil remaining milk and pour on to the blended mixture. Return to pan and simmer, stirring continuously. Add sugar; cover, and allow to cool.

2 with eggs (good for children)
1 pint milk
3 eggs
4 oz castor sugar

Heat the milk. Beat together the eggs and sugar. Add the hot milk slowly, stirring continuously. Return to the pan and cook without boiling until custard coats the back of a wooden spoon. Strain, cover and cool.

BASIC (VANILLA) ICECREAM

1 economical
¼ pint cream or prepared evaporated milk
1 pint cold icecream custard
1 teaspoon vanilla essence

Half whip the cream or evaporated milk. Add the custard and vanilla. Chill and freeze.

6 helpings. Time 2½ hours.

2 refrigerator iced mousse
2 level teaspoons icing sugar
1 gill cream
2 egg whites
  vanilla essence

Sieve the icing sugar. Whip the cream, and add 1 tablespoon of the sugar. Stiffly whip the egg whites and fold in the other tablespoon of sugar. Mix together carefully the cream, egg whites and vanilla. Turn into a tray and freeze in the ice-making compartment of the fridge for half an hour. Remove the tray and whisk the mixture till mushy. Return it to the tray, and finish freezing it.

Other essences and flavourings can be used instead of vanilla in all the recipes above.

BURNT ALMOND ICECREAM

2 oz loaf sugar
2 oz almonds
1½ pints icecream custard
¾ gill cream
1 tablespoon kirsh
  (optional)

Blanch, shred and bake the almonds until brown. Put the sugar and a few drops of water in a saucepan and boil until it acquires a deep golden colour. Add the cream, boil up and stir into the custard. Chill, add the almonds, and the kirsh, if used, and then freeze the mixture.

MILK SHAKES

1 pint milk
2 scoops icecream
2 tablespoons flavouring
essence or fruit juice and
sugar

Method 1
Stir the flavouring into the milk; add the icecream just before serving.

Method 2
Mix together all the ingredients; chill. Remove from refrigerator, beat thoroughly and serve while still frothing.

2 glasses.

Most children enjoy ending their meal with a colourful dessert gâteau. Give them spoons to eat it with:

APRICOT GÂTEAU

9 oz dried apricots
1 pint water
3½ oz castor sugar
lemon juice to taste
9 oz sponge fingers or
trifle sponges
¼ pint double cream,
sweetened

This superb gâteau is made in a baking tin, about 8 × 4½ inches in size. Make the gâteau at least 24 hours in advance, as it should be kept in a cool place for a whole day. Leave the washed apricots to soak overnight. Simmer them the next morning until they are soft. Leave them to drain and cool, then rub them through a sieve or blend in an electric blender until smooth. Mix the purée with the sugar and with lemon juice to taste. Line the cake tin with aluminium foil. Place one layer of sponge fingers on the bottom and cover them with the apricot pulp. Fill the tin with alternate layers of biscuits and pulp, ending up with a layer of biscuits. Leave the gâteau for 24 hours in the refrigerator. Turn the gâteau out just before serving, and remove the foil. Whip the double cream stiffly and decorate the top.

MOCHA GÂTEAU

4 oz butter (preferably
unsalted)
10 oz castor sugar
4 eggs
10 oz self-raising flour
1 small teaspoon salt
4 oz melted plain chocolate
¼ pint cold strong black
coffee
½ pint double cream
icing (see recipe for
biscuits with names)
chocolate glaze

Combine butter, sugar and yolks of eggs and cream thoroughly. Sift flour and salt together and add gradually to the mixture, together with the coffee and melted chocolate. Lastly fold in the stiffly beaten egg whites. Pour the mixture into a well-greased and lined round 9-inch cake tin. Bake in a moderate oven, at 180° C, 350° F, Gas Mark 4 until cooked. This takes about 1 hour. When cold, cover all over with icing and drizzle with chocolate glaze.

CHOCOLATE GLAZE

2 oz plain chocolate
1 tablespoon water, coffee
or rum
½–2 oz unsalted butter

Stir the chocolate and liquid in a bowl set over a pan of very hot water until the chocolate dissolves. Remove from the heat and beat in the butter a tablespoon at a time. Stand the bowl on ice or in a pan of cold water until cooled. Beat again. When it reaches the consistency you want, spread or drizzle the glaze on your cake.

BASIC BISCUIT RECIPE (Shrewsbury Biscuits)

4 oz butter or margarine
4 oz castor sugar
1 small egg
8 oz plain flour
½ level teaspoon ground
   cinnamon or grated lemon
   rind
milk as required

Cream the fat and sugar and beat in the egg. Sift the flour with the cinnamon, or add grated rind, and add to the creamed fat mixture. Mix to a stiff consistency, using milk if required. Roll out fairly thinly and cut out with a 2½-inch cutter. Place on a greased baking sheet and bake in a moderate oven (180° C, 350° F, Gas Mark 4) till a light fawn colour.

30–32 biscuits. Cooking time 15–20 minutes.

for the icing
3½ oz sieved icing sugar
1 tablespoon water or
   orange juice, strained
   orange colouring
   biscuits of different
   shapes

Sieve the icing sugar carefully, and stir in the water or orange juice gradually until you have a smooth icing. Keep it stiff as you will use it for piping. Fill a forcing bag with icing, and pipe the name of each little guest, and naturally the name of the birthday child, on each biscuit. Leave to dry, and use them as name place markers on the plates of the guests.

Lastly, don't forget the sweets:

TOFFEE APPLES

1 lb sugar
4 oz butter
2 tablespoons water
12 apples

Wash the apples and put a clean stick into each so that it feels firm. Put all the ingredients for the toffee into a strong saucepan and allow the sugar to dissolve very slowly over a low heat. Boil to the 'small crack' degree (290° F). Dip each apple into cold water, then into the toffee and then into the cold water. Put on to an oiled slab or buttered paper to set. Use immediately as they go sticky on keeping.

CHOCOLATE ALMONDS

chocolate
vanilla essence
almonds, blanched and dried

Dissolve the chocolate in the smallest possible quantity of hot water and flavour it to taste with vanilla essence. Dip each almond in separately and place them on an oiled slab or plates to set.

CREAM CARAMELS

1 lb sugar
1½ gills water
¼ lb glucose
1 oz butter
1 gill cream
   caramel essence

Dissolve the sugar in the water, add the glucose, and boil to 265° F. Then add the butter and cream, and stir until the mixture again registers 265° F. Remove from the heat, flavour to taste, and pour on to a well-oiled tin. When sufficiently firm, mark with a caramel cutter or knife.

When quite cold cut into squares, wrapping them in waxed paper.

parties for teenagers

Any parent with teenage sons or daughters must be well aware of the fact that everything they think, do or organize may well be thought old-fashioned, ridiculous, stiff or dull, and that they have no idea what is 'in' at the moment. The young may even hint or say outright that, when a party is in the offing, then parents should stay out of it, completely out of it.

Some parents, of course, interfere too much, and suggest shocking limitations. Others 'fall for' their youngsters' attitude and go out for the evening. Both courses are unwise. But the latter is more so. Gossip will tell them later, 'that party lasted until six in the morning . . . and the whole night the record player was at full blast . . . and they were allowed to use all the china and furniture . . . and dancing lasted until the morning . . .'

Sometimes these tales are used by the teenagers themselves, as a way to impress, as they were in your own youth. But there is usually no smoke without a small fire below. So do not give way concerning certain rules and standards. Do your utmost to make sure that the youngsters have a pleasant time, and leave them to themselves as much as possible, but keep, invisibly, an eye on things. Even party behaviour has to be learned by experience by young people.

There is always a chance too that parental background help is approved and even appreciated, and that afterwards the youngsters are even grateful, because the party was a success.

The first problem to be solved in a teenage party is the space. If one has a garage, an attic or a usable cellar, then the space problem is solved. It is more difficult if no such place is available. You may be prepared to vacate your living-room for the evening; but be wise and remove beforehand all articles which are dear to you. The youngsters will approve of that themselves — they have no use for your nice carpet and easy chairs.

The decoration is best left to the youngsters themselves. After all, it is their party and you will lack the fantasy they have in such abundance. You may even be shocked by the pictures, posters, drawings or what not they want to display. Nevertheless the best thing you can do is to laugh about it.

You may be required to provide some technical assistance, and no doubt they will want to borrow various items. Ironing-boards make excellent sideboards if covered with crêpe paper. Harsh electric bulbs in cellar or garage are hidden behind coloured paper. One can even hang up paper Chinese lanterns. 'Real' Chinese lanterns with candles are totally wrong, as in the excitement they are bound to catch alight. Boxes can be up-ended to make seats covered with pieces of foam rubber, which in turn are hidden by old curtains or coloured plastic bags.

Large coloured Mexican paper flowers are extremely effective decorations. They are, of course, rather expensive, but can be used again. Alternatively, some enormous red poppies or sunflowers from the excitingly coloured tissue papers which are available. Three of those mounted on wire and displayed in a bottle or jar, form a gay decoration.

Nobody in his right mind offers his best china and glasses for use at a teenage party. The most suitable 'glasses' are the plastic picnic beakers which can be thrown away afterwards.

There is also nothing better available than plastic cardboard plates either. They are cheap and pleasant and prevent upheavals about broken china afterwards, as well as squabbling over the washing up. Talking about clearing up: it must be made clear from the start that things must be cleared up afterwards. A garage or attic can remain untidy until next day, but the living-room must be returned to a 'liveable' condition. You may help with the tidying up, but on principle the youngsters should do it themselves.

Finally, warn your neighbours that you are organizing a party which will involve a lot of noise.

drinks and snacks

Drinks and snacks for a teenage party must be simple. The main question is: how much? and only later: how nice? Food and drinks are not the most important part of a teenage party. The atmosphere, the music and dancing are far more important.

A common bone of contention between parents and offspring is whether or not to serve alcoholic drinks. One has to be extremely careful. In some groups, strong alcoholic drinks such as gin, vodka and cognac are quite normal at teenage parties. But parents who object and are steadfast in saying that they will not allow it in their homes, are right. Strong alcoholic drinks have no place at a teenage party. Not all the youngsters have yet learned the effects of alcohol, and some of the inexperienced ones may be going to drive home. This is a perfect reason to give for not permitting strong drink. If one of them crashes his motor cycle or car, it will be your responsibility.

Beer and light wines are quite another matter. Most teenagers have probably become acquainted with these at home, and will know how to treat them at a party. Indispensable, too, are long drinks! Provide large quantities of fruit juices and tonic or ginger ale. Consult the young people, however, before you make a 'cup' or punch. Most teenagers prefer their drinks 'straight'.

Beer needs no further explanation, but don't forget the idea of serving shandy, half beer, half ginger ale and lemonade.

Talking about mixing beer in the other drinks, a festive drink for older teenagers is:

BLACK VELVET

Combine equal parts of dark beer and a sparkling wine (for example, a Luxembourg vin perlé).

mixed drinks

Perhaps there are enthusiastic 'mixers' amongst the party-goers. Let them go ahead behind an ironing-board 'bar'. Super drinks can be prepared from non-alcoholic drinks. There are plastic cocktail shakers on the market which do not cost much, and which serve the purpose if making:

GRAPE COCKTAIL

Equal parts grape juice and orange juice. Shake with ice cubes, serve and fill the glass up with tonic water.

125

CITRUS COCKTAIL

Equal parts of lemon juice, orange juice and pineapple juice. Mix in the shaker with ice cubes.

TOMATO COCKTAIL

Mix in the shaker 1 part tomato juice, half a part lemon juice, a dash of Worcester sauce, a pinch of celery salt, and a pinch of pepper. Serve with ice cubes.

If long drinks are more popular, these too can be prepared by the 'bartender' behind his ironing-board.

CINDERELLA

The base is the citrus cocktail, which is served in tall glasses, filled up with a fruit drink.

FRUIT LONG DRINK

Orange juice in the bottom of the glass, which is then filled up with raspberry or cherry juice; float a pineapple ring or cube on top, or a sprig of mint. A few drops of Angostura bitters in the fruit juice improve this drink.

MIMOSA

Fill half the glass with orange juice, and fill up with Luxembourg vin perlé.

CITRUS GINGERADE

A layer of orange juice first, followed by ginger ale.

All these drinks must be well chilled. Fruit juices can be stored in buckets of cold water, if possible with ice cubes in the water.

snacks

The snacks at teenage parties must be easy. Save your masterpieces for your own parties. At a teenage evening, they are completely wasted.

The best thing to provide is large platters with tasty tit-bits: peanuts, potato crisps and salties are favourites. Large red and white cabbages can be cut level at the bottom so that they can stand steady upright; stick cocktail picks in them, displaying a colourful array of 'bits': cheese cubes, sausage cubes, small cocktail onions and gherkins. To make it more interesting, add the cheese cubes, pieces of ginger or pineapple, and to the sausage ones, cocktail onions or pieces of pickled cucumber.

Also put out bowls of the dip sauces, described in an earlier chapter, and the breads to go with them.

Let us also give you some ideas about more substantial snacks, which will do you honour:

POTATO SALAD WITH SAUSAGES

Cube hot, newly boiled waxy potatoes, and mix with a good salad cream mixed with some very finely chopped onion and freshly ground pepper. Serve with cocktail sausages or frankfurters.

RICE SALAD WITH TUNA

Mix cooked rice with finely chopped vegetables and redbell pepper, as well as cubed tuna. Spoon mayonnaise over the dish and decorate with slices of hard-boiled egg and radish.

ENGLISH MEAT BALLS

Make freshly minced meat savoury with grated onion, salt, pepper, paprika, parsley and a dash of Worcester sauce. Bind with a panada or egg-yolk. Make into small balls and fry in margarine or dripping over a low heat, turning the balls to brown them all over. Stick them on cocktail picks and place them on a platter in the centre of which you put a bowl of tomato sauce, or condensed tomato soup, which you have heated without diluting it.

BEAN SAUSAGES

Warm small cocktail sausages and place them on cocktail sticks on a platter. In the centre of the dish, put a bowl of peanut sauce (see below).

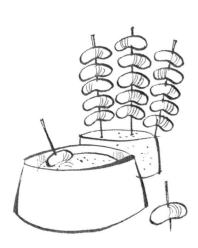

PEANUT SAUCE

Fry finely chopped onion in hot oil, stir in a jar of peanut butter, add a very little chilli or Tabasco sauce and 1–2 tablespoons vinegar. Then dilute with water.

DUTCH BITTERBALLEN (MEAT BALLS)

The best thing to use for these is well-cooked stewing beef, minced. Make a thick ragoût sauce; melt 1½ oz butter, and mix in 2 oz of flour. Cook for 2–3 minutes, then add 1 pint stock or bouillon. Leave to thicken and season with salt, pepper, curry powder and monosodium glutamate. Stir in the finely minced beef. Leave to cool. Then shape into small balls, dredge with flour, and toss in beaten egg yolk. Finally, roll them about on paper covered with golden breadcrumbs. Fry them in fat until golden-brown.

Lastly, in water, provide for the end of the party, vacuum flasks of hot soup!

parties for the family

There is an old proverb which says that a life without celebrations is like a road without ports of call. Yet we still like to have a reason for a party, and luckily events within the family circle usually manage to provide them.

There are of course the annual excuses of Christmas and Easter. But every family also has its very own private parties, which the children remember and repeat when their generation is the adult one. So these parties become like golden clasps tying together the volumes of years.

Besides these, within our own span, we have an annual string of birthdays, and also our own moments of glory when our children pass their examinations, when the little ones achieve something very special, the 75th birthday of a grandfather or grandmother, father's promotion, the introduction of a future son or daughter-in-law. Some of the more romantic among us traditionally celebrate their own wedding anniversary. Then, although there are many families in which weddings are celebrated in a hall, there are still couples who prefer (and can use) the intimacy of a home.

On the following pages we describe some suggestions for a luncheon, a wedding breakfast, a simple evening get-together, a reception and a dinner, all in the intimate atmosphere of the home. You can use them, adapted, for various occasions; and you will find other ideas in the earlier chapters, many of which have been dealing with parties at home.

the table

Whatever the occasion, the laid table should sparkle with a festive air, even before a single dish has been put on it. This does not mean that just anything goes, however — the table decorations should underline the celebration, by being in the same style.

A classic luncheon or dinner table for instance may be polished and bare or laid with a snow-white damask tablecloth; and the floral decoration consists of low, vases of pastel flowers. Beautiful indeed, but perhaps somewhat dull! We prefer a gayer, more colourful approach, as long as it is in good taste and harmonious.

A delicately coloured tablecloth is excellent for a celebration at home, provided the colour is in harmony with the dinner service, the flowers and the candles.

China with a blue decoration looks perfect on a pale pink or pale yellow cloth, provided there are yellow or pink candles in the candlesticks and the flowers are a composition of blue and pink or blue and yellow. Multi-coloured china looks best on a white cloth or on a plain cloth in one of the colours of the design and the floral decoration is then also kept in one colour. If the china is white, or perhaps white with a narrow golden edge, one can use any pale- or dark-coloured cloth, if the flowers are in colours which tone in.

Do not place a high centrepiece on the table; it only restricts the view across the table. If the table is small, use two candlesticks in the centre and only a very small floral decoration. On an oblong table two or three tiny bowls of flowers or pot-pourri look attractive.

For preference, do not use strong-smelling flowers as a table decoration — hyacinths, for example! They will overpower the wine. Small chrysanthemums are suitable; anemones, or rosebuds. In springtime, you can make glorious combinations of narcissi and various other small flowers. On the annual celebration of your wedding anniversary, use only a few red roses. . . .

a luncheon

When the main point of the celebration comes around midday (for example after a church ceremony) then we all get together at a festive luncheon.

A classic lunch is always lighter than a dinner, and usually consists of a light first course, a clear soup, a light meat course, such as chicken or veal and a dessert.

Weddings take place at many times of day and different kinds of parties follow them. But a morning wedding is often followed by a luncheon.

In France they sometimes call the after-wedding meal a 'dejeuner-dinatoire' to indicate that this lunch combines two meals. In England, however, it is a fairly light repast like a classic lunch.

At a 'dejeuner-dinatoire', the menu above is usually extended to include another hot first course or a fish dish after the soup, and cheese before the dessert. At the end of the meal, however, comes the famous cutting of the wedding cake.

A classic luncheon or wedding breakfast menu could consist of:

OYSTERS 'AU NATUREL'

•

MIMOSA SOUP

•

VOLS-AU-VENT

•

BREAST OF VEAL À LA AUVERGNE

•

ALOHA ICECREAM

With some careful planning, this menu can be prepared so fully that the housewife need only spend a short time in the kitchen at the last moment. The recipes are all designed for 6 people.

a wedding breakfast

OYSTERS AU NATUREL

To eat 'au naturel' all that is needed, after being opened, is the oysters to be placed on the upper shell with a little of the liquor; they are then arranged on a dish, garnished with sprigs of fresh parsley, and, if possible, surrounded with ice. Thin slices of buttered brown bread, quarters of lemon and Tabasco sauce can be handed round at the same time; also cayenne pepper and vinegar.

It is advisable to ask the fishmonger to open the shells for you.

MIMOSA SOUP

2 pints clear stock or canned consommé
3 large eggs
1 8-oz pkt frozen green beans

Make sure the stock or consommé is quite free from grease. Hard-boil the eggs. Cut the beans into paper-thin strips. Bring the soup almost to boiling point. Scatter in the beans, then the yolks of the eggs, finely crumbled. Serve with salted biscuits.

VOLS-AU-VENT

Vol-au-vent or patty cases filled with savoury mixtures are excellent for first courses and also for buffet parties. They can be served hot or cold. If a mixture is being put into cold pastry cases, make sure it is quite cold. If, on the other hand, it is being put into hot pastry cases, heat the filling and the pastry separately, and put together at the last minute, so that the filling does not make the pastry soft.

Vol-au-vent cases can be bought uncooked, frozen, or ready to use. They can also, of course, be made at home, using frozen or home-made puff pastry.

HOT VOL-AU-VENT

Hot vols-au-vent cannot have fillings which melt easily and run out of the casing. Here are types of fillings from which you can develop others:

chicken filling
1 3-oz pkt full fat soft cheese
1 chicken joint, cooked
1 small onion, peeled and sliced

Divide the cheese into six portions (for 6 vols-au-vent). Cut the chicken into bite-sized pieces. Fry the onion rings gently until tender.

In six vols-au-vent, lay (a) onion rings (b) a little cheese. Add the chicken and remaining cheese. Heat vols-au-vent in a gentle oven.

bacon and mushroom filling
**6 rashers streaky bacon
1 3-oz pkt full fat soft
  cheese
¼ lb mushrooms, sautéed in
  butter
salt and pepper**

Chop the bacon and fry until crisp. Chop the mushrooms and add them. Season, and cool.

Mix half the cheese with the bacon bits, and half with the mushrooms. Spread bacon and cheese in the lower halves of six vols-au-vent. Fill the upper half of each vol-au-vent with the mushroom–cheese mixture. Top with vol-au-vent 'hats'. Toast or heat as in previous recipe.

BREAST OF VEAL À LA AUVERGNE

**2¼ lb breast of veal
2 slices of bread without
  crusts
1 finely chopped onion,
  lightly fried
1 tablespoon parsley,
  chopped
7 oz chestnut purée,
  unsweetened
pepper, salt
large piece of bacon rind
  or pork skin with some
  fat on it
½ bottle white wine
1–2 onions, chopped
2–3 carrots, chopped
1 bunch parsley stalks
1¾ oz butter**

When ordering the veal, tell the butcher you want to stuff it. Make a stuffing of the bread, soaked in a little water and squeezed, the fried onion, parsley and chestnut purée. Stuff the breast and tie with string. Season. Place the bacon rind or pork skin in a shallow casserole or covered roasting pan, fatty side up. Place the meat on top. Baste with melted butter and the wine, arrange the onions, carrots and parsley stalks round it, and cover the pan closely with the lid or with foil. Place the pan for 2½ hours in a moderate oven, at 180°C, 350°F, Gas Mark 4. Remove from the pan, cut into slices, and serve with other vegetables such as chestnuts and French fried potatoes.

ALOHA ICECREAM

**1 pint vanilla icecream
1 15-oz can pineapple pieces
3 tablespoons crème de
  menthe liqueur
3 egg whites
pinch of salt
7 oz icing sugar**

Place the chopped pineapple in a large flameproof dish and sprinkle with the liqueur. Beat the egg whites until very stiff with the salt. Add the sugar gradually, still beating. Just before serving, place the icecream on the pineapple, cover with the meringue and put in an oven heated to 220°C, 425°F, Gas Mark 7 for a moment or two, to brown the meringue slightly.

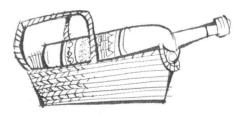

the wine

Only light wines are served at a luncheon or a wedding breakfast. The classic and most festive is, of course, champagne. If you choose a dry one, you can serve it right through the meal given above.

A CONTINENTAL WEDDING CAKE

1 lb 5 oz flour
1 lb 2 oz sugar
1 lb butter
8 eggs
1 oz baking powder
⅛ pint Curaçāo liqueur
10 tablespoons milk
1 lb 2 oz finely chopped
  glacé fruit or candied peel
  icing sugar
  Maraschino liqueur as
  required
  silver balls (bought)
  pink and white sugared
  almonds (bought)

Today many young couples turn down the idea of a traditional fruit wedding cake covered with marzipan and hard icing, developed for its keeping quality (since the first tier can be kept for the first child's christening). The cake below will keep well enough to be sent to absent friends, and may be a pleasantly novel one.

Beat the butter with the sugar until soft. Add the eggs one by one, beating well between each addition. Sift in the flour and baking powder mixed; when half the quantity has been added, trickle in the milk. Do not stop beating. Add the rest of the flour mixture. and beat well before adding the liqueur and fruit. Transfer the mixture to three cake tins, all buttered, and graduated in size, and bake the cakes at 170° C, 325° F, Gas Mark 3, until done. Cool on a wire rack. Make a glaze with the icing sugar and Maraschino liqueur. Cover the tops of the three cakes, and place one on top of each other. Cover the whole assembled cake. Place silver balls and sugared almonds in a pattern on the cake while the glaze is still slightly soft. In the centre of the top tier, place a small vase for tiny white flowers.

An informal evening 'get-together' will present few problems. If it is to celebrate an old people's Golden Wedding or a grandparent's birthday, for instance, it can be kept very simple, with tea and a special cake, followed by a drink; before returning home, a cup of coffee and an open sandwich will be welcome. Some people take the opportunity to serve home-made:

FRUIT IN BRANDY

Use only sound fruit; wash it carefully and leave it to drain. For 2 lb fruit (apricots, peaches, morello cherries or plums) you require 1 lb sugar, a piece of cinnamon stick and 2 cloves. Place the fruit in well-sterilized jars, pour the brandy on it, add the sugar, cinnamon and cloves. The fruit must be well covered with liquid. Seal the jars tightly with a glass stopper or screwed-on lid. Leave for some weeks in a cool, dark place.

Do not over-feed your guests: quality is better than quantity. If you want to serve wine, leave the cake until afterwards; most wines do not taste well as a rule with sweet food. It is better to serve savoury snacks with the wine, such as cheese, pâté, ham or sausage rolls. Then, with the coffee, serve your sweet delicacy or special cake.

Take care that your drinks are well served: beer and spirits should be cold, and so should white wine; a rose wine or red wine should be at room temperature.

the reception at home

Family events may be celebrated by a formal reception but, of course, the guests include friends and others outside the family circle. Among family events, a reception is usually given for an engagement, a wedding or (rarely) an important wedding anniversary. More and more formal receptions are being held in an hotel, since at home there is just not adequate space to receive large numbers of guests. However, if your house is a large one it is more pleasant to organize an important celebration at home, especially a formal engagement. This is organized by the parents of the girl. Wine may be served at a reception, or sherry, port, white or red vermouth and spirits such as whisky and gin. Savouries, cheese biscuits and similar snacks are served with them. It is quite usual for the guests to want to sit down for a short time, so provide some small chairs, and a few hot snacks for those who have a long journey home. Sweet snacks can be combined with white port or sweet white vermouth. Don't forget the petits-fours, which do not require plates.

ARTICHOKE HEARTS

canned artichoke hearts
small pastry cases, vols-au-vent or round canapés
mayonnaise
salt and freshly ground pepper to taste
mustard to taste
grated onion to taste
finely chopped parsley to taste

Leave the artichoke hearts to drain (there are usually 12 in a can) and then marinate them for 1–2 hours in mayonnaise to which the flavourings have been added. Place one artichoke heart in a case or on a canapé, and sprinkle some finely chopped parsley on top. The base or canapé must remain firm, so do not make this snack too early.

Hot snacks include:

STUFFED MUSHROOMS

2 lb mushrooms
1 lb cream cheese
2 tablespoons dry sherry
salt to taste
freshly ground pepper

Buy fairly large mushrooms of equal size. Wipe them clean with a dry cloth and remove the stems. Mix the cream cheese with the sherry, salt and pepper and cover the mushroom heads with it. Served with a cocktail pick this is a simple snack to make. Some people prefer the mushroom parboiled, but take care that they remain firm, and drain them well.

PETITS-FOURS

2 egg whites
4 oz ground almonds
2 oz castor sugar
a few drops almond essence
rice paper
glacé cherries
angelica

Whisk the egg whites very stiffly, and fold in gradually the mixed almonds and sugar. Drip in the almond essence as you work. Place the mixture in a forcing bag with a large decorative pipe and force it on to rice paper in rosettes or oblongs. Decorate with tiny pieces of glacé cherry or angelica and bake in a moderate oven (180° C, 350° F, Gas 4) until golden-brown. They take about 20 minutes.

20–30 small petits-fours.

dinner after the reception

After the reception, there often follows a dinner just for the family. Some extra help is essential for this, however simple you keep the menu. After all, the hostess can hardly be present at the reception and keep an eye on things in the kitchen at the same time. The following menu could serve for this type of dinner, or for any other formal celebration dinner.

GRAPEFRUIT COCKTAIL
•
TURTLE SOUP
•
VEAL ROSE WITH HARICOTS VERTS
•
ICECREAM GÂTEAU
•
COFFEE

GRAPEFRUIT COCKTAIL

A canned grapefruit cocktail is very simple. Just remove the sections from the can, place them in a champagne glass and decorate with a cocktail cherry. Don't pour on the traditional sherry or kirsch, but use Aquavit, which is surprisingly pleasant.

TURTLE SOUP

Turtle soup is one of the most tasty canned soups, which only has to be warmed (just below boiling point) and poured into very small cups. Good advice: never dilute this soup, as it will spoil the typical flavour. You can add a dash of Madeira to it.

VEAL ROSE

4 slices of veal each
  salt
  freshly ground pepper to
  taste
1 oz butter
  a dash of olive oil
  a glass dry vin rose
  a little flour
$\frac{1}{4}$ pint double cream

The recipe is for 4 persons and must be adjusted to the number of guests. Season the meat with salt and pepper and coat it with flour. Fry them briefly in the butter and oil on both sides over moderate heat, until slices are golden-brown on both sides. Remove the veal from the pan and place it in a flameproof dish. Pour the wine into the pan and you will get a thin sauce; slightly thicken it with a little extra flour if you wish. Season again if necessary with salt and pepper. Pour the sauce over the veal slices and place them in a very low oven, where they can wait until serving time. Just before serving, place on each slice a tablespoon of double cream, which has been partially whipped. Sometimes the veal slices are also served with a slice of lemon on top. The rose wine best suited to this meat dish is Tavel, which should be at cellar temperature.

As for the green beans, buy either canned, frozen or dried ones for convenience. Warm them with some butter when prepared and serve with freshly boiled baby potatoes if you wish.

Icecream gâteaux are increasingly popular. Rather than trouble yourself, buy a ready-made one, which you can keep in your freezing compartment of the refrigerator.

Coffee and liqueurs make a worthy end to this formal but light meal.

In memory of the good times together, some couples like to repeat their engagement dinner at their silver wedding. On these occasions, the dinner is longer, since a silver-wedding cake is served with the dessert or after it. In this case, a good replacement for the icecream gâteau is:

CERISES FLAMBÉES

1 pint vanilla icecream
1 15-oz can morello cherries without stones
$\frac{1}{8}$ pint cognac, kirsch or Drambuie liqueur

Place a scoop of firm icecream in a coupe glass for each guest. Drain the cherries over a small saucepan. Heat the cherry liquid, sweeten if required and add the spirit. Quickly top the icecream with the cherries. Light the warmed (not hot) liquid and pour over the cherries at the moment of serving.

Easter joy

At this time of year, we think of lambs and Easter chicks, and Easter's egg dishes. Pick a warm spring afternoon to do your Easter shopping if you can. The parks show signs of spring; go-ahead supermarkets, greengrocers and health stores boast their first bunches of fresh herbs. Perhaps you will spot some fresh fennel or chervil, borage and basil to take home, and a few fennel roots to use as a celebration vegetable.

POACHED EGGS WITH CREAM SAUCE

4 fresh eggs
1½ oz butter
2 dessertspoons flour
½ pint lukewarm milk
salt
pepper
nutmeg
4–6 tablespoons double cream
3–4 tablespoons Parmesan cheese
1 tablespoon ready-made Dijon mustard
dry breadcrumbs

Make the following sauce for the 4 eggs. Melt the butter in a heavy saucepan. Stir in the flour until smooth. Add the lukewarm milk gradually, and continue stirring. Season with a pinch of salt, pepper and nutmeg. Leave to simmer for 5–10 minutes on a very low heat. Stir in the cream, and then the cheese and mustard; stir for another 2–3 minutes. Taste and add more salt if necessary. Poach the eggs in poaching pans or boiling water. Place some of the hot sauce in 4 individual earthenware dishes. Put a poached egg into each dish and cover with the remaining sauce. Scatter some dry breadcrumbs on top and place the little bowls in a hot oven or under the grill for about half a minute.

OMELET WITH CHICKEN LIVERS

3 eggs
double cream
butter
½ lb chicken livers
1 tablespoon finely chopped onion
salt and pepper
paprika to taste
1 clove of garlic, squeezed
extra butter

If you eat chicken for your dinner at night, it may be a good idea to use the livers for lunch.

Make an omelet of three eggs in a 6½-inch frying pan. For this, mix the eggs with a little cream, but do not overbeat. Only slightly season an omelet if you are going to fill it. Don't use too much butter, and always use a flexible spatula. Hold the handle of the pan in your left hand and the spatula in your right. As the edges of the omelet solidify, turn them over and let the still liquid substance flow underneath; with your left hand give the pan a slightly twisting turn. After filling, use the spatula to fold over the one half over the other half of the omelet before it is entirely solidified, and slide the omelet on to a pre-heated plate. Never fry an omelet on both sides.

For the filling, fry the chicken livers together with the other ingredients in butter until golden-brown. You can make the filling beforehand and keep it warm, until you want to fill the omelet.

LAMB CUTLETS WITH ONION

2 oz finely diced bacon
2 oz finely chopped onion
2 oz finely sliced carrot
1 chopped leek
  parsley, thyme and bay
  leaf
1½ oz butter
1 pint boiling milk
  pepper and salt
1½ oz butter
1½ oz flour
3–4 onions
  butter as required
  pepper and salt
  nutmeg
  cayenne pepper, a pinch
  only
  icing sugar, a pinch only
6–8 lamb cutlets
  butter
  grated cheese
  Madeira

Make the onion sauce first; call it, if you want to be more sophisticated, 'sauce soubise'. Start with a Béchamel sauce, the basis for many other sauces. It is a blond sauce, and not, as so many cookbooks tell you, one made only with butter, milk and stock. You need more ingredients for a good Béchamel; but do remember that it is not necessary to use all the sauce at once, as it keeps well for a day or two in the refrigerator. Cook the first 6 ingredients for 15 minutes in 1½ oz butter as a mirepoix. Add the boiling milk, or half milk and half stock. Season with salt and pepper and leave to simmer for 15 minutes. Rub through a sieve.

Make a white roux in a heavy saucepan: melt 1½ oz butter on low heat; stir in the flour with a wooden spoon. Stir in the strained mirepoix, and leave to simmer for 15 minutes. This is a true Béchamel sauce.

Blanch the peeled onions for 3 minutes in boiling water, remove them, dry them and chop them. Brown quickly in butter; this improves the flavour. Purée the onions in an electric blender, or by sieving.

Add ½ pint onion purée to ½ pint Béchamel sauce for the sauce soubise, and simmer it to thicken to the consistency you want. Season with pepper and salt, nutmeg, a pinch of cayenne pepper and a pinch of icing sugar.

Fry the slightly peppered and salted cutlets until brown. Remove them from the saucepan and cover them with a thick layer of onion sauce. Sprinkle some grated cheese on top and leave them to brown in a hot oven.

Thin the pan juices with a spoonful or two of Madeira. Serve with French bread and a light salad of lettuce, blanched strips of celeriac, sections of orange, olive oil, a little lemon juice, fresh herbs, pepper and salt and rub the salad bowl with garlic.

ROAST CHICKEN

1 baby chicken for each
  person

and for each chicken
salt and pepper
aluminium foil
1 slice lean bacon
  garlic, squeezed
5 baby onions
1 sliced carrot
  finely chopped fresh herbs
  butter, in ½-inch cubes

Season the inside of each chicken with salt and pepper and place each one on an ample piece of aluminium foil. Cover each with one slice of lean bacon and some garlic; surround with baby onions, sliced carrot and plenty of finely chopped herbs. Add some cubes of butter and neatly seal the foil. Slide the parcels into a moderate oven, at 180° C, 350° F, Gas Mark 4, and leave for about half an hour or a little longer. Open the parcels and leave open in the oven to brown the chickens. Serve with buttered brown bread.

CROWN ROAST OF LAMB

2 best ends of neck of lamb
butter
pepper
salt
2 cloves of garlic, squeezed
1 shallot, minced
4 tomatoes, skinned and
puréed
stuffing of your choice
(see recipe)

Ask your butcher to prepare this joint. Its crown shape is achieved by turning outward two best ends of neck, which are then trussed and skewered together to form a circle. The centre of this roast can be stuffed with spiced minced meat, diced mixed vegetables or savoury rice; and along the inside edge you can drape a string of chipolata sausages.

Place the crown in a baking tray, and roast in a moderate oven, heated to 180° C, 350° F, Gas Mark 4. Baste it with the butter.

The roasting time will depend on the thickness of the meat and the type of stuffing. Season with the remaining ingredients by shaking or pouring them over the meat shortly before the end of the cooking time. Be careful with the seasoning: the stuffing and sausages will be seasoned already.

Leave the crown in the turned-off oven to firm up while you make the gravy.

Finish the gravy with some reduced clear stock and a glass of white wine, rose or cognac. Before serving, crown the top bones with cutlet frills. Serve the crown on a heated dish surrounded by a variety of vegetables such as garden peas, cauliflower rosettes, asparagus tips and French beans. Serve fried, sautéed or matchstick potatoes. A dry rose wine is excellent with this dish.

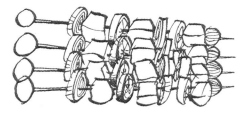

ROAST LAMB KEBABS

2 lb 10 oz leg of lamb
parboiled onions, sliced, as
required
tomatoes, sliced, as
required
parboiled greenbell
peppers, cubed, as required
ground dill
pepper and salt
Malayan Spiced Dressing
(see recipe)

Use fairly long skewers, preferably the large kind butchers use. Cut the meat into 32 cubes; and on each skewer, thread the meat and vegetable pieces in this order: onion, meat, tomato, meat, onion, meat, green pepper, meat, onion.

For the Malayan Spiced Dressing, make a dipping sauce or dressing of olive oil, vinegar, soy sauce, cayenne pepper, paprika and tomato ketchup, used in proportions which suit your palate.

Brush the kebabs with the dressing and grill them on all sides until dark brown, repeating the brushing occasionally.

Christmas

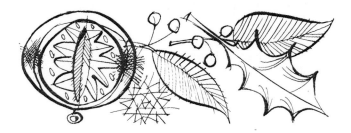

Christmas! So rich in traditions, especially in its menu, where we are bound to find roast turkey or goose, beef or pork! On the following pages you will find some more unusual suggestions for the Christmas dinner from various parts of the Continent. Use them instead of (or to supplement) your Christmas holiday meals.

POLISH CARP

1 onion ⎫
1 carrot ⎬ all finely chopped
1 leek ⎭
  parsley
  bay leaf
1 carp
6 peppercorns
  salt to taste
  sugar, a pinch only
2 oz butter
1½ oz flour
¼ pint red wine
1 tablespoon raisins
6 dried prunes, soaked and
  stoned
1 thick slice honey cake or
  light gingerbread
1 tablespoon chopped
  blanched almonds
  salt
  pepper
  juice of 1 lemon
  pinch of sugar
6 slices of lemon

Place the finely chopped vegetables and the herbs in a large saucepan. Leave them to simmer in about ½ pint of water. Put the cleaned carp on top, season with peppercorns, salt and sugar. Let it cook gently for about one hour. Remove the carp, strain the liquid and replenish with red wine to make 1 pint. Keep the carp warm. Melt the butter, stir in the flour, fry gently, then gradually add the red wine sauce. Add raisins to this sauce and the prunes (cut in pieces), the crumbled honey cake and almonds. Leave to simmer for about 20 minutes. Season with more salt, a pinch of pepper, lemon juice and a pinch of sugar. Place the carp, decorated with lemon slices, on a large platter and pour the sauce round it.

Serve with macaroni, baked in butter, with sesame seeds on top, and with beetroot salad mixed with soured cream and with crumbled hard-boiled egg on top.

BAKED HAM (for 8 persons)

1 3–4-lb piece of ham on
   the bone
2 cloves
   bouquet garni
3½ oz butter
1 carrot, cut in strips
1 onion, cut in strips
   thyme
1 bay leaf
6 peppercorns
   half a bottle red wine
   icing sugar to sprinkle
   wine sauce (see recipe)
   stock
12 cloves

Soak the ham overnight. Change the water, add the cloves and bouquet garni and bring to the boil. Keep the water at a temperature just below boiling point, and cook the ham gently, skimming well for 1–1¼ hours. When the ham is cooked, strip off the skin. This is easily done by lifting the corner carefully with a knife and then pulling off with the fingers. If the ham has come straight from the pan and is very hot, hold the skin with kitchen paper or a cloth.

Melt the butter in a baking tin with a cover, place the vegetables in it, also the thyme, bay leaf and bruised peppercorns. Set the ham on the vegetables, fatty side up, pour on the red wine, cover and leave the ham to braise for about an hour in a low oven, at 150° C, 300° F, Gas Mark 2. Take the ham out of the oven and dust with icing sugar. Turn the oven up to 200° C, 400° F, Gas Mark 6, and replace the ham in the oven to caramelize the sugar. Take the ham out and score the top. Place a clove in each square. Place the ham on a serving dish. Strain all the juices, add a little stock and thicken with cornflour if you wish, to make the wine sauce.

ROAST GOOSE WITH RED CABBAGE (10 persons)

1 young goose
7 oz dried apples
7 oz dried prunes
1 tablespoon grated lemon
   rind
   salt
   pepper

Leave the apples and prunes to soak overnight. Stone the prunes. Chop both prunes and apples. Mix in the lemon rind, and stuff the goose with this apple–prune mixture. Seal the opening with poultry skewers. Rub the goose with salt and pepper, place on a grid, and place this grid in the baking tin, so that the goose cannot fry in its own fat. Pour a beaker of boiling water over the goose and place the bird in a moderate, pre-heated oven at 180° C, 350° F, Gas Mark 4, for 3–3½ hours. Baste the goose occasionally. If the fat becomes very hot, add some water.

For the red cabbage, use:

1 small red cabbage
1 oz margarine
1 onion chopped very
   finely
2 cooking apples
1 tablespoon golden syrup
   juice of ½ lemon
2 tablespoons vinegar
   salt
2 cloves
1–2 teaspoons ground
   cinnamon

RED CABBAGE

Melt the fat. Add the onion and fry gently until light brown. Add the cabbage finely shredded, the peeled and sliced apples, and the spices and syrup. Cook over very gentle heat for 10 minutes, shaking the pan frequently. Add lemon juice, vinegar, and salt and simmer covered for 1–1½ hours. Stir occasionally. Season and serve.

6 helpings.

Christmas menu 1
(for 6 persons)

HAM CREAMS

•

BEEF BROTH WITH GOLDEN ROLL SLICES

•

TURKEY WITH CHESTNUTS AND
CRANBERRIES

•

CHRISTMAS PUDDING WITH RUM SAUCE

HAM CREAMS

nearly $\frac{1}{2}$ pint double cream
tablespoon lemon juice
tablespoon Madeira
6 oz cooked ham
1 8-oz can crushed pineapple
parsley
$\frac{1}{2}$ pint mayonnaise
$\frac{1}{2}$ oz gelatine
salt
pepper
grated onion

Whip the mayonnaise with the cream, lemon juice and Madeira. Add onion. Add the gelatine. Leave the mixture to set a little, then add the finely chopped ham, pineapple and parsley. Transfer the mixture to small individual containers which have been rinsed with cold water. Leave to set and chill in the refrigerator. Turn them out on to small plates. Decorate with lettuce, onions and gherkins. Serve with toast and butter.

BEEF BROTH WITH GOLDEN ROLL SLICES

1 carrot
1 turnip (small)
1 onion
salt and pepper
$\frac{1}{2}$ small cabbage
a sprig of parsley
1 clove of garlic (optional)
1 oz butter or margarine
1 qt brown stock
a few chives
grated nutmeg
6 thin slices of French bread

Scrub and peel the carrot and turnip, peel the onion and crush the garlic (if used). Slice the vegetables in thin rounds. Melt the fat and in it cook the vegetables gently for 10 minutes with a lid on the pan. Add the stock (boiling) and $\frac{1}{2}$ teaspoon salt. Simmer the whole for 30 minutes.

Meanwhile wash the cabbage, shred it finely and chop the parsley and chives. Add the cabbage to the broth and simmer for 20 minutes longer; then add seasoning, a little grated nutmeg, and the chopped parsley and chives. Toast or bake the slices of French bread till golden-brown and put one in each soup plate or cup; pour the hot soup over them. If liked, grated cheese can be handed round with this soup.

TURKEY WITH CHESTNUTS AND CRANBERRIES

1 turkey
2–3 lb chestnuts, dried or
fresh
$\frac{1}{2}$ pt chicken stock
2 oz butter
1 egg
salt and pepper
cream or milk
1–1$\frac{1}{2}$ lb sausage meat or 1 lb
veal forcemeat
2–3 slices bacon
fat for basting
gravy

If fresh, slit the chestnut skins, cook them in boiling water for 15 minutes, drain and remove the skins. If dried, soak overnight, then simmer 15 minutes in fresh water.

Stew the prepared chestnuts in stock for 1 hour; drain, and then chop or sieve them, keeping a few back for garnish. Make the stuffing with the chopped chestnuts, butter (melted), egg, seasoning and cream. Fill the crop of the bird with this stuffing and the body with sausage meat, well seasoned. Truss the bird for roasting. Cover it with bacon, and roast in a moderate oven (180° C, 350° F, Gas Mark 4) until tender, basting well. Towards the end of the cooking time, remove the bacon to let the breast brown. Remove the trussing string before dishing the bird. Garnish with the reserved chestnuts, and serve with gravy and cranberries.

CHRISTMAS PUDDING
(rich, boiled)

10 oz sultanas
10 oz currants
$\frac{1}{2}$ lb raisins
2 oz sweet almonds
   (skinned and chopped)
1 level teaspoon ground
   ginger
$\frac{1}{2}$ lb plain flour
   pinch of salt
1 lb soft brown sugar
$\frac{1}{2}$ lb mixed finely chopped or
   candied peel
1 level teaspoon mixed spice
1 level teaspoon grated
   nutmeg
$\frac{1}{2}$ lb breadcrumbs
10 oz finely chopped or
   shredded suet
6 eggs
$\frac{1}{2}$ gill stout
   juice of 1 orange
1 wine glass brandy
$\frac{1}{2}$ pint milk (approx)

Grease three 1-pint pudding basins. Prepare the dried fruit; stone and chop the raisins; chop the nuts.

Sift the flour, salt, spice, ginger and nutmeg into a mixing bowl. Add the sugar, breadcrumbs, suet, fruit, nuts and candied peel. Beat the eggs well and add to them the stout, orange juice and brandy, and stir this into the dry ingredients, adding enough milk to make the mixture of a soft dropping consistency. Put the mixture into prepared basins. Cover and boil steadily for 6–7 hours. Take the puddings out of the water and cover them with a clean dry cloth and, when cold, store in a cool place until required.

When required, boil the puddings for $1\frac{1}{2}$ hours before serving.

3 puddings (each to give 6 medium helpings).

RUM SAUCE

1 pint milk
   peel of $\frac{1}{2}$ lemon
2 oz sugar
$\frac{1}{2}$ oz cornflour
2 egg yolks
$\frac{1}{4}$ pint rum

Bring the milk to boil with the lemon peel. Leave to simmer for a few minutes. Remove the peel, add the sugar. Remove the milk from the heat and cool it a little while stirring. Thicken the milk slightly with the cornflour. Whisk the egg yolks, add a little of the warm milk and mix well; pour the mixture into the remaining milk. Finally stir in the rum. Heat very gently until thickening. Serve warm.

Christmas menu 2
(for Boxing Day)

GARDEN PEA SOUP

•

RABBIT WITH PRUNES

•

FROZEN TANGERINE MOUSSE

GARDEN PEA SOUP

½ lb deep-frozen garden
   peas
3 pints whitestock
1 teaspoon dried mint
1¾ oz raw ham, cubed
   pinch of sugar
   salt
   pepper
2–3 tablespoons double
   cream

Simmer the garden peas in the stock with the dried mint for a few moments. Rub the peas through a sieve. Add to this lovely pale green soup, the cubed ham and seasoning, and leave to simmer for another 5–10 minutes. Add the cream. Sprinkle chopped parsley on top and serve with fried bread cubes.

RABBIT WITH PRUNES

1 rabbit
   salt
   pepper
   ground thyme
3½ oz butter
   flour
12 small onions, peeled
3½ oz lean bacon, diced
¼ pint white wine

Cut the rabbit into 4 parts. Rub them with the salt, pepper and thyme and pass them through the flour. Melt most of the butter, place the bacon and onions in the pan and fry quickly. Remove them from the pan and place the rabbit in the pan to brown quickly on all sides. Add the remaining butter. Add the wine, bacon and onions and leave the rabbit to simmer for another hour or so, occasionally adding a little water or more wine. Alternatively, cover the dish tightly and leave for 3–4 hours or overnight in the oven at the lowest possible heat. This dish reheats well if you cook it ahead, to save work on the day.

PRUNE COMPOTE

1 lb dried prunes
½ pint red wine
   a few drops of cognac
4 tablespoons sugar
   pinch of cinnamon
   cornflour

Leave the prunes to soak overnight in the wine and cognac, then simmer them in this liquid over low heat with the sugar and cinnamon. Thicken the sauce with cornflour, after removing the prunes.

FROZEN TANGERINE MOUSSE

8 tangerines
4 oz sugar
2 egg whites
¼ oz gelatine
½ pint water

Remove the tops of the tangerines and scrape out the flesh. Rub this through a sieve and measure the quantity. You should have approximately ½ pint fruit pulp, if not, make it up with orange juice. Boil the sugar and water to a light syrup and dissolve the gelatine in this. Mix in the tangerine pulp and leave to cool. When at setting point, add the beaten egg whites and freeze in the ice compartment of the refrigerator (at its coldest setting), stirring occasionally with a fork to keep the icecream light. Leave frozen overnight if you wish.

The tangerine skins should have also been placed in the cold compartment so that they are cold and firm. Shortly before serving, place the tangerine mixture in the skins and decorate with stiffly whipped cream, or with red and green candied fruit. Place the tangerines in couples on a plate, or set in a quick-setting glaze.

traditional parties

New Year's Eve

After a year interlaced with a string of festivities, both official parties as well as intimate home parties, we approach the end of the year — and the beginning of a new one.

Why not try doing it the continental way, with apple dumplings or fritters and a traditional hot mulled wine?

HOT MULLED WINE

2 bottles red Bordeaux
2 oranges
1 lemon
20 cloves
$\frac{1}{8}$ pint cognac
   sugar to taste

Pour the wine into a saucepan. Wash the oranges and lemon and stick the cloves in their skins. Leave the wine to simmer for 10 minutes on a very low heat — take care that it does not boil. Just before serving, add the cognac, remove the fruit and stir in the sugar to taste.

This manly hot wine is, of course, not intended for the very young. You could heat the wine in two pans and provide only one with cognac. The hot wine goes very well with the traditional fairly heavy, sweet foods of the evening.

This sweet start to a continental New Year's Eve changes to savoury dishes around midnight. This savoury assembly can be as varied as you choose, ranging from various snacks and salads to an extensive supper, which, in its turn, can range from a cold buffet to a complete hot meal.

Whatever you decide to do, take care that all is ready just before midnight. This means that the drinks, which must be served chilled and at room temperature, must also be ready, the wine bottles must be uncorked so that the host can pour out just before midnight and all your guests can drink to the New Year at the stroke of twelve.

153

FRITTERS WITH YEAST

¼ oz yeast
¼ teaspoon castor sugar
1½ gills warm milk (approx)
6 oz plain flour
  pinch of salt
1 oz melted butter

Cream the yeast and sugar, and add a little milk. Sift together 2 oz of the flour and salt into a warm bowl. Mix to a batter consistency with the yeast mixture, adding more milk if required. Leave to rise until doubled in bulk. Add the rest of the flour and warm milk, work in and add the melted butter. Leave to rise again, in a warm place for quick rising or low down in the fridge overnight. After coating, fritters made with yeast batter should stand for 30 minutes on buttered paper before being fried.

Sweet fritters can be divided into those made with fruit or other solid ingredients, such as stale cake or bread, and those made with loose or near-liquid foods such as raisins, rice or jam. Fruit can be fresh, frozen or canned; it may be plain, or soaked in a syrup or liqueur before coating. Stones (e.g. prune stones) *must* be removed from fruit before coating.

Fritters should be dredged with castor sugar just before serving.

VARIOUS TYPES OF FRITTERS

Apple Fritters   2 apples, cored and sliced; coating batter; castor sugar for dredging; lemon wedges as accompaniment.

Apricot Fritters   2 canned apricot halves, drained coating batter; castor sugar mixed with ground cinnamon for dredging.

Banana Fritters   4 firm bananas, cut lengthwise and across; coating batter; castor sugar for dredging.

Bread and Butter Fritters   6 thin jam sandwiches without crusts; coating batter; castor sugar mixed with ground cinnamon for dredging.

Orange Fritters   4 oranges, peeled and without pith, in pieces of 3–4 segments; coating batter; castor sugar for dredging.

BAKED APPLES OR APPLE DUMPLINGS

6 cooking apples
2 oz demerara sugar
½ gill water
pastry (optional)

fillings
2 oz moist sugar and
2 oz butter

blackcurrant or raspberry or strawberry or apricot jam

3 oz stoned dates or sultanas or currants or raisins, 2 oz soft brown sugar and 1 teaspoon ground cinnamon

Prepare the filling. Wash and core the apples. Cut round the skin of the apple with the tip of a sharp knife, two-thirds of the way up from the base. Put the apples into a flameproof dish and fill the centres with the chosen filling. Sprinkle with the demerara sugar. Add the water. Bake in a moderate oven (180° C, 350° F, Gas Mark 4) until the apples are soft in the centre – about ¾–1 hour depending on the cooking quality of the apples.

To make baked apple dumplings   Stuff the apples after peeling and coring them. Use 12 oz short crust pastry if they are big apples, 8 oz if they are small. Cut the pastry into 6 pieces, and roll out in rounds. Work a piece of pastry round each apple, and seal with a little water. Place the dumplings, join side down, on a greased baking sheet. Brush with milk, dredge with castor sugar and bake at 200° C, 400° F, Gas Mark 6 for about 30 minutes.

NEW YEAR COOKIES

2 oz margarine
1½ oz sugar
¼ egg
4 oz plain flour
pinch of salt
½ level teaspoon powdered cinnamon
¼ level teaspoon baking powder
a little jam

decoration
glacé cherries
icing using 3 oz icing sugar

Cream the fat and sugar, add the egg. Sift the dry ingredients and work into the fat mixture. Mix to a stiff consistency and roll out thinly. Cut into 2–2½-inch rounds and bake in a moderate oven (180° C, 350° F, Gas Mark 4). When cold, put 2 together with jam, coat with the icing and decorate with pieces of cherry or a spot of red colouring.

12–16 biscuits. Cooking time 20 minutes.

about
the photos

measures used in this book

The dry goods and liquids in this book are measured either in ounces and pounds (or table and teaspoons) or in gills and pints.

16 tablespoons fill a 10-fluid-ounce measuring cup. One tablespoon holds 3 teaspoons.

Oven heats are given as Celsius (centigrade), Fahrenheit and Gas Mark numbers.